Ian Hobday is a senior lecturer in Economics at the South Downs College of Further Education, Havant, having previously been Head of Economics at King's Heath School, Birmingham.

He is co-author of *Pan Study Aids: Commerce*.

Pan Study Aids for GCSE include:

Accounting

Biology

Chemistry

Commerce

Computer Studies

Economics

English Language

French

Geography 1

Geography 2

German

History 1: World History since 1914

History 2: Britain and Europe since 1700

Human Biology

Mathematics

Physics

Sociology

Study Skills

PAN STUDY AIDS

ECONOMICS

I. L. Hobday

A Pan Original
Pan Books   London and Sydney

First published 1987 by Pan Books Ltd,
Cavaye Place, London SW10 9PG

9 8 7 6 5 4 3 2 1

© I. L. Hobday 1987

ISBN 0 330 29985 9

Text design by Peter Ward
Text illustration by M L Design
Photoset by Parker Typesetting Service, Leicester
Printed and bound in Spain by
Mateu Cromo SA, Madrid

CONTENTS

6   Contents

Contents 7

8   Contents

INTRODUCTION TO GCSE

From 1988, there will be a single system of examining at 16 plus in England, Wales and Northern Ireland. The General Certificate of Secondary Education (GCSE) will replace the General Certificate of Education (GCE) and the Certificate of Secondary Education (CSE). In Scotland candidates will be entering for the O grade and standard grade examinations leading to the award of the Scottish Certificate of Education (SCE).

The Pan Study Aids GCSE series has been specially written by practising teachers and examiners to enable you to prepare successfully for this new examination.

GCSE introduces several important changes in the way in which you are tested. First, the examinations will be structured so that you can show *what* you know rather than what you do *not* know. Of critical importance here is the work you produce during the course of the examination year, which will be given much greater emphasis than before. Second, courses are set and marked by six examining groups instead of the previous twenty GCE/CSE boards. The groups are:

> Northern Examining Association (NEA)
> Midland Examining Group (MEG)
> London and East Anglian Group (LEAG)
> Southern Examining Group (SEG)
> Welsh Joint Examinations Council (WJEC)
> Northern Ireland Schools Examination Council (NISEC)

One of the most useful changes introduced by GCSE is the single award system of grades A–G. This should permit you and future employers more accurately to assess your qualifications.

GCSE	GCE O Level	CSE
A	A	–
B	B	–
C	C	1
D	D	2
E	E	3
F	F	4
G		5

Remember that, whatever examinations you take, the grades you are awarded will be based on how well you have done.

Pan Study Aids are geared for use throughout the duration of your courses. The text layout has been carefully designed to provide all the information and skills you need for GCSE and SCE examinations – please feel free to use the margins for additional notes.

NB Where questions are drawn from former O level examination papers, the following abbreviations are used to identify the boards.

UCLES	AEB
ULSEB	SUJB
O & C	SCE
JMB	SEB

PREFACE:
ECONOMICS AT GCSE

GCSE ECONOMICS SYLLABUS CONTENT

The syllabus content of the six examining groups is essentially the same. You should, however, be aware that there are differences between the boards in approach and content detail. Students will need to study syllabuses and specimen papers to gauge these differences.

Here is an outline of different syllabuses which you can use as a guide to syllabus content.

GCSE ECONOMICS – THE DIFFERENT SYLLABUSES IN OUTLINE

London & East Anglia	Midland	Northern	Southern	Welsh	Northern Ireland
1. The fundamental economic problem: scarcity	1. The basic economic problem: choice	1. Scarcity	CORE:	1. Introduction – micro and macro problems	1. The fundamental economic problems of scarcity and choice
2. The price system	2. The nature and functions of UK organizations and institutions	2. Households – demand, supply and allocation	1. The nature of economic problems	2. The pricing system	2. The allocation of scarce resources within different types of economic systems
3. Enterprise: its forms, scale and organization	3. How the market works	3. Firms – demand, supply and allocation	2. Interdependence	3. Population	
4. Location of industry	4. The individual as producer, consumer, saver and borrower	4. Government – demand, supply and allocation	3. Allocation	4. Labour economics	3. Supply and demand
5. Financial institutions	5. The private firm as producer and employer		4. Economic decision-making	5. Industrial economics	4. The organization of production. Economies of scale
6. Public revenue and expenditure	6. The role of government in the UK economy		5. Income and wealth creation and distribution	6. Financial economics	5. Industrial location
7. Macroeconomics: prices, employment, income and growth	7. Interdependence and conflict between the aims of firms and government		6. National economic issues	7. International trade	6. Money and banking
8. Trade	8. A description of recent changes and trends in the UK economy and a simple analysis of their consequences		OPTION I: SOCIAL ECONOMICS:	8. Personal economics	7. Stock Exchange
9. Factor markets			1. The individual as consumer	9. Current economic issues	8. Labour and trade unions
10. Population: structure, distribution and change			2. The individual as producer		9. Public sector
			3. The individual as a citizen		10. International trade
			OPTION 2: ECONOMIC PRINCIPLES:		11. National income
			1. Production		12. Unemployment
			2. Money and banking		13. Inflation
			3. National income		14. Population
			4. Economic policy		
			5. International economic issues		

ASSESSMENT TECHNIQUES

All the examining groups use four main assessment techniques:

(a) **Short-answer questions** (perhaps data-based) These may be of the multiple-choice type of question or open-response short-answer questions (i.e. one/two sentences in response to the question).

(b) **Data-response questions** Questions are set on a prose passage or table of statistics, pie diagrams or photographs.

(c) **Extended writing questions** These may be essay-type questions or extended structured questions (perhaps data-based).

(d) **Coursework** This will be internally set and may be essay-based.
     Each group differs in the weighting it gives to each of the four main types of assessment technique and the time allocated to each. Some papers involve compulsory questions in the paper.

Here is a guide to the assessment techniques employed by the different groups. Students need to refer to a copy of an economics specimen paper of the group for which they are sitting the exam.

ASSESSMENT OBJECTIVES

In the four main assessment techniques the examining groups are attempting to satisfy broadly five assessment objectives. These are that candidates will be expected to
(*a*)   demonstrate recall of knowledge in relation to a specified syllabus.
(*b*)   demonstrate an ability to use this knowledge in verbal, numerical, diagrammatic, pictorial and graphical form.
(*c*)   demonstrate an ability to explain and apply appropriate terminology, concepts and elementary theories.
(*d*)   select, analyse, interpret and apply data.
(*e*)   distinguish between evidence and opinion, make reasoned judgement and communicate them in an accurate and logical manner.

GCSE ECONOMICS ASSESSMENT

London and East Anglia	Midland	Southern	Wales	Northern	Northern Ireland
Paper 1 (2½ hours) SECTION A: Compulsory short-answer questions. 15% of total marks. 15/20 minutes SECTION B: 2 compulsory data-response questions 20% of total marks. 30/35 minutes SECTION C: Extended writing question, structured and data-based. Choose 3 from 7. 40% of total marks. 1½ hours **Paper 2** Coursework. Three assignments of 500–1,000 words each. 25% of total marks	**Paper 1** (1 hour) 40 multiple-choice questions. 25% of total marks **Paper 2** (2 hours) SECTION A: 2 compulsory data-response questions SECTION B: Extended writing questions, structured and data-based. Choose 2 from 5. 50% of total marks **Coursework** Choose 3 units from 5 prescribed topics, not more than 1,000 words. 25% of total marks	**Paper 1** (1 hour) 40 multiple-choice questions. 30% of total marks **Paper 2** (2 hours) PART 1: 2 compulsory data-response questions and one structured essay question (from a choice of 3). 30% of total marks. Based on syllabus core PART 2: 1 compulsory data-response question and 1 structured essay question (from a choice of 3). 20% of total marks. Based on syllabus option **Paper 3** Coursework. 2 units of 750–1,000 words. 20% of total marks	**Paper 1** (2½ hours) SECTION A: Compulsory short answer questions. Maximum of 45 minutes. 24% of total marks SECTION B: 2 data-response questions. Maximum of 45 minutes. 24% of total marks. SECTION C: 2 structured essay questions from a choice of 6. Minimum of 60 minutes. 32% of total marks **Paper 2** Internally assessed coursework. Either field work or project work. 20% of total marks	**Paper 1** (2½ hours) SECTION A: Between 30 and 40 short-answer questions. 30 minutes. 15% of total marks SECTION B: Between 4 to 7 questions which may be structured essay type and data response. 55% of total marks **Coursework** Candidates will be required to submit 1, 2 or 3 assignments involving investigation outside the classroom. The number of words will be no more than 3,000 in total. 30% of total marks	**Paper 1** (1½ hours) 12 compulsory short-answer questions **Paper 2** (2 hours) 5 compulsory structured and data-response questions **Paper 3** (1½ hours) SECTION A: 1 compulsory data-response question SECTION B: 2 structured extended writing essay questions from a choice of 4 **Coursework** 1 assignment of 1,000 words maximum

ECONOMIC PROBLEMS AND SYSTEMS

CONTENTS

The basic economic problem is that of scarcity of resources. All other economic problems derive from this. We will begin this book by explaining the meaning of the basic problem. This chapter is divided into the following sections:

1   **The basic economic problem** Wants are greater than scarce resources. This means that goods and services are scarce. Consumers have to make a choice, and this involves an opportunity cost.

2   **Some important definitions** Economics consists of many words and phrases which we need to define quite clearly.

3   **The factors of production** There are four factors of production – labour, land, capital and enterprise.

4   **Alternative economic systems** Three main types of economy have developed in an attempt to solve the basic economic problem. These are the market economy, the planned economy and the mixed economy. This section discusses how each economy operates and their respective advantages and disadvantages.

1   THE BASIC ECONOMIC PROBLEM

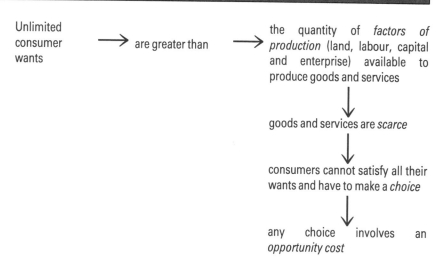

The diagram above illustrates the basic economic problem which underlies all economic problems. It is this problem which all economic systems are attempting to overcome.

Consumers wants are unlimited. This means that consumers (i.e. anybody who buys or purchases) want food, shelter, clothes, etc. These wants are unending. For instance a consumer may want food, then more food and better food.

Goods and services cannot, however, be produced in unending amounts because the factors of production (or resources) are themselves limited in supply. Therefore goods and services are scarce (which means limited in supply).

Consumers may decide to satisfy some of their wants but this will mean that other wants may go unsatisfied. This choice will involve an opportunity cost, which is the best alternative choice which has been forgone. For instance, a consumer may have to decide whether to go on a foreign holiday or purchase a new car.

If the consumer decides to purchase the new car, then the opportunity cost is the foreign holiday forgone. Opportunity cost is often referred to as the real cost of making a choice. It does not apply only to individual consumer choices but also to community choices. For example, a community may decide to build more roads and fewer hospitals. The opportunity cost of the new roads is the lack of hospitals.

2 SOME IMPORTANT DEFINITIONS

(i) **Production** . . . the process of creating goods and services which consumers are prepared to consume to satisfy their wants. The production process involves the use of the factors of production – land, labour, capital and enterprise – without which production could not possibly take place.

(ii) **Producer** . . . a creator of goods and services.

(iii) **Consumption** . . . the process of consumers using goods and services because it gives them satisfaction and satisfies their wants.

(iv) **Consumer** . . . a user of the created goods and services.

(v) **Goods** . . . tangible and visible commodities, e.g. cars, washing machines, food, clothes.

(vi) **Services** . . . intangible and invisible commodities, none the less produced, e.g. health and education services.

(vii) **Commodities** . . . all goods and services

(viii) **Producer or capital goods** . . . those goods produced to produce other goods and services, e.g. machinery and factories.

(ix) Consumer goods . . . those good produced to give immediate satis-faction to consumers, e.g. food, TVs, videos.

(x) Durable goods . . . those consumer goods which have a relatively long life, e.g. motor-cars, videos and washing machines.

3 THE FACTORS OF PRODUCTION

The quality and quantity of production depends on the quality and quantity of available resources. By resources is meant the factors of production: labour, land, capital and enterprise.

(a) LABOUR

Labour is the mental and physical human effort involved in the production process. Economists and politicians regard labour with special concern because it involves human beings. Labour earns an income or reward called *wages*. Labour is dealt with in more detail on pp.121–3.

(b) LAND

Land has a wide definition in Economics. It includes all kinds of natural resources such as farmland, raw material deposits, climate, forest and fishing grounds. Owners of land earn a reward or income called *rent*.

(c) CAPITAL

Capital is not the same as money. In Economics, capital comprises all those resources required not for their own sakes but because they produce other commodities. It would include factory premises, machinery, raw materials in stock, transport vehicles and partly finished goods.

Social capital includes all capital which belongs to the community, such as schools, hospitals and libraries. Owners of capital earn a reward or income called *interest*. Refer to pp.132–3, the section on wealth.

(d) ENTERPRISE

Enterprise is the factor of production which brings together the other three. The *entrepeneur* is the organizer who decides what is to be produced, where and how. Without the entrepeneur the other resources have no economic importance – they need to be brought together and organized for production. The functions of the entrepeneur include management and control and risk (uncertainty) bearing. This distinguishes enterprise from labour, because the entrepreneur carries the risks of production. If the entrepreneur makes successful decisions then a *profit* is the reward or income received. Of course, bad decisions can result in losses. The entrepreneur need not be an individual – it could be the government. (See Chapter 6.)

Now answer the following multiple-choice questions:

MC1 Which of the following is best described as a producer good?
(*a*)   a television
(*b*)   a foodstuff
(*c*)   a lorry
(*d*)   a fish
(*e*)   a washing machine

MC2 All the following are factors of production except a
(*a*)   factory manager
(*b*)   tractor
(*c*)   company share
(*d*)   shop assistant
(*e*)   teacher

MC3 'If we build more hospitals and schools this year it means we must have fewer houses.' To an economist this statement illustrates the concept of
(*a*)   opportunity cost
(*b*)   elasticity of demand
(*c*)   diminishing returns
(*d*)   utility
(*e*)   occupational mobility

MC4 The factor of production known as land is usually defined as
(*a*)   land on which factories are built
(*b*)   land used for cultivation only
(*c*)   land which contains raw materials
(*d*)   land used for building and cultivation
(*e*)   the surface of the earth together with its natural resources

MC5 If a firm decided to stop manufacturing Product X and to produce Product Y instead, the opportunity cost to the firm of this would be the
(*a*)   revenue obtained from Product Y
(*b*)   costs incurred by manufacturing Product Y
(*c*)   increased revenue expected from Product Y
(*d*)   revenue lost from Product X
(*e*)   original cost of developing Product X

4 ALTERNATIVE ECONOMIC SYSTEMS

The basic economic problems faces all economies, and each country will attempt to allocate its scarce factors of production (resources) in the most efficient method possible. Three main economic systems have developed, each attempting to allocate scarce resources efficiently: The market economy system, the planned economy system and the mixed economy system.

(a) THE MARKET ECONOMY SYSTEM

There are various other terms for the market economy which the examiner may use: the capitalist economy, the price economy, the unplanned economy, the *'laissez-faire'* economy (*'laissez-faire'* is French for 'leave it alone') and the private enterprise economy. A market economy does not exist in its purest form in the world today, but the USA is the nearest example.

(i) THE ALLOCATION OF SCARCE RESOURCES

Scarce resources are allocated without any government interference. The market (i.e. producers and consumers) decides what will be produced. Consumer wants are transmitted to the producers (or entrepreneurs) by price signals. This means that if consumers want apples, demand for apples increases, the price of apples increases and, because apple production is more profitable, producers produce and supply more apples. Scarce resources are allocated by private entrepreneurs to apple production. Of course, events can run in the opposite direction. A fuller account of the operation of the market mechanism will be found in Chapter 2.

(ii) ADVANTAGES OF THE MARKET ECONOMY

–   There is no state interference in the economic system. There is no need for a large civil service.

–   Consumers are said to be sovereign. This means that consumers are very powerful in the market economy, deciding what goods and services will be produced. Price is their signal to producers.

–   In a market economy many small entrepreneurs exist, producing a large variety of different goods and services.

–   The market economy is efficient because the main objective of entrepreneurs is to make a profit. To do this they must allocate resources efficiently.

–   Competition between many different entrepreneurs will lead to lower prices for consumers.

–   Economic freedom coexists with political freedom for consumers. The government keeps out of people's lives.

(iii) DISADVANTAGES OF THE MARKET ECONOMY

–   Private entrepreneurs would not produce certain goods and services which may be unprofitable. However, for social (or cultural or educational) reasons these goods and services should be provided, e.g. library services, education for low-income families, museums, etc.

–   Private entrepreneurs should not produce certain goods and services because this may be dangerous. For instance, if a private entrepreneur was allowed to manufacture (unregulated) nuclear weapons this could give him (or her) much power.

–   In a market economy there will be an inevitable inequality in income and wealth distribution. Some entrepreneurs and workers will work harder or be luckier than others. This could be seen as unfair.

–   The better-off individuals will exercise a great deal of market power because they will be able to demand certain luxury commodities. Thus scarce resources may be allocated to producing, say, champagne and caviar, to the exclusion of bread and potatoes.

–   Some small entrepreneurs will be more successful than others. Gradually industries will become dominated by a small number of entrepreneurs. Eventually a single producer will exist (called a monopoly) who will be able to determine prices and output because there is no competition.

–   The market economy does not run as smoothly as its supporters indicate. There will be time-lags as some industries run down and others expand. Workers will be unemployed and may be unwilling to move into other jobs, especially if these jobs are in another area of the country.

(b) THE PLANNED ECONOMY SYSTEM

There are various other terms for the planned economy which the examiner may use: the command economy, the collective economy and the communist economy. The planned economy does not exist in its purest form in the world today, but the Soviet Union and other communist countries in Eastern Europe (and elsewhere) are near examples.

(i) THE ALLOCATION OF SCARCE RESOURCES

Scarce resources are allocated by the government. State planners decide what will be produced, where and how. The bureaucrats (civil servants) are the entrepreneurs and are not motivated by profit. The market mechanism does not play a role. Consumer wants may be ignored and private entrepreneurs are not allowed. The Soviet Union, for instance, plans its economy in a series of Five-Year Plans, setting production targets for a variety of industries.

(ii)　ADVANTAGES OF A PLANNED ECONOMY SYSTEM

– 　The government can ensure a more equal distribution of income and wealth.

– 　Goods and services which would not (or should not) be provided by the market economy system may be provided by a planned economy concerned about social, educational and cultural developments.

– 　Scarce resources can be allocated to the production of necessities – e.g. basic foodstuffs – not luxuries.

– 　The planners can ensure, as some industries expand and others decline, that there is a smooth reallocation of resources.

– 　The wastes and duplications of the market economy can be avoided, e.g. many small firms producing roughly the same good or service can be prevented.

– 　Private monopolists, (see pp.81–3) who may exploit consumers with high prices, will not exist.

(iii)　DISADVANTAGES OF A PLANNED ECONOMIC SYSTEM

– 　Planners may not know consumer wants and may make wrong decisions, leading to a shortage of some goods and services and a surplus in others.

– 　Without a profit motive workers and managers have no incentive to work hard.

– 　Many bureaucrats are needed to run the system. These are an extra cost to the consumers. Also, many planners may be frightened to make decisions in case of mistakes.

– 　The government decides what is a luxury and what is a necessity. However there is sometimes a difference of opinion about what is a necessity/luxury, e.g. is a car a luxury or a necessity?

– 　Planned economic systems allocate a large proportion of scarce resources to producing a capital goods and not consumer goods. This means present-day consumers have a lower standard of living.

– 　A lack of economic freedom coexists with a lack of political freedom. The state interferes in almost every aspect of human life.

(c)　THE MIXED ECONOMY SYSTEM

The mixed economy system includes aspects of both the market system and the planned system. To some extent all economies are mixed, differing only in the degree of market and planning involved. For instance, the US economy is mainly a market economy but the state does interfere to raise taxes, to spend on schools and welfare and, indeed, to defend the country. Similarly, the Soviet Union economy is mainly planned but aspects of the market economy can be found in agriculture – Russian agricultural workers can sell any surplus on the open market.

The United Kingdom is a good example of a mixed economy, with a private enterprise sector and a public enterprise sector. Much of the UK economy is left to private entrepreneurs, but government interference is to be seen in taxation and government spending, the armed forces, education, health and the welfare state and the nationalized industries.

Now answer the following multiple-choice questions:

MC6 In a fully planned economy, who decides what will be produced?
(*a*)   private entrepreneurs only
(*b*)   government only
(*c*)   consumers only
(*d*)   the government in public enterprise and consumers in private enterprise
(*e*)   the government in public enterprise and private entrepreneurs in private enterprise

MC7 In a market economy prices are determined by
(*a*)   consumers
(*b*)   manufacturers
(*c*)   government
(*d*)   the forces of demand and supply
(*e*)   the costs of production

For multiple-choice questions **MC8**, **MC9** and **MC10**, select your answers from the following code:

if 1 only is correct	A
if 1 and 2 only are correct	B
if 3 and 4 only are correct	C
if 2, 3 and 4 only are correct	D
if 1, 2, 3 and 4 are all correct	E

MC8 Which of the following is/are characteristic of mixed economies?
1   subsidies for some industries
2   the operation of the market economy in parts of the economy
3   government control of some industries
4   private entrepreneurs motivated by profit-making in some industries

MC9 Which of the following is/are true of a planned economy?
1   resources are allocated by government plans and commands
2   there is a more unequal distribution of income and wealth
3   private monopolies exist
4   workers and managers are motivated solely by profits

MC10   Which of the following can be included in the economist's definition of land?
1   building land
2   forests
3   fishing grounds
4   crude oil deposits

EXTENDED WRITING QUESTIONS

1   'The reason wants are not satisfied is that there is a lack of resources called factors of production.'
(a)   Briefly describe the factors of production.
(b)   What is meant by the problem of scarcity of resources?
(c)   What do you consider to be the most important factor of production? Explain your answers.

2   (a)   The basic problems of scarcity of resources underlie all economic problems. Explain this statement.
(b)   Illustrate, with the use of an example, the principle of opportunity cost.
(c)   Distinguish between capital goods and consumer goods. Give three examples of each type of good.
(d)   Why does an economy seek to acquire capital goods?

3   (a)   In what ways do command economies and market economies differ?
(b)   Outline the workings of the price mechanism in a market economy.
(c)   Outline three advantages of a market economy.

Answer
To answer (a) you need to discuss the main differences between planned and market economies. You need to stress the main differences between them. They attempt to overcome the basic problem of scarcity of resources in different ways. The market economy uses the market forces of demand and supply, the government does not interfere (*laissez-faire*), resources are allocated by private entrepreneurs motivated by profit (price is the signal). Theoretically the consumer is sovereign.

A planned economy, on the other hand, allocates resources through planning by government bureaucrats. Planners decide how, where, when and what is to be produced. Profit does not play a role.

To answer (b) you need to show the workings of demand, supply and price in allocating scarce resources. It would be useful to illustrate your ideas with a graph. Stress the role of consumers (consumer sovereignty) and producers motivated by profit. The government does not interfere (*laissez-faire*).

The answer to (c) can be found on p.21, where we have discussed the advantages of the market economy. Note the question requires only three advantages.

4   (a)   What are the main features of a planned economy?
    (b)   What criticisms are often made of such an economic system?
    (c)   Outline three advantages of such an economy.

5   (a)   How does a market economy allocate scarce resources?
    (b)   Why is the UK economy considered to be a mixed economy?
    (c)   Discuss the merits and demerits of a mixed economy.

DATA RESPONSE

The community expresses its *wants* through spending decisions, i.e. by being willing to spend so much on particular goods. Business responds to these decisions by allocating *scarce resources* to produce the *goods and services* required by the consumer. Thus in this system it is the consumer who makes the decision, and that is why you may sometimes hear the expression the *'consumer is king'*. (Terry Price, *Basic Economics* (Pan))

(a)   Explain the meaning of the words and phrases in italic in the passage.
(b)   What is meant by the basic economic problem of scarcity of choice?
(c)   (i) The extract is a description of what type of economic system?
       (ii) Give three advantages and three disadvantages of this type of economy.
(d)   (i) 'The UK is a mixed economy.' Explain the meaning of this statement.
       (ii) How are scarce resources allocated in a mixed economy?
(e)   (i) Explain how the balance of the mix in the UK's mixed economy has changed in the last 10 years.
       (ii) Give reasons for these changes.

Answers to multiple-choice questions:

MC1	(c)		MC6	(b)
MC2	(c)		MC7	(d)
MC3	(a)		MC8	(e)
MC4	(e)		MC9	(a)
MC5	(d)		MC10	(e)

PRICE, DEMAND AND SUPPLY

CONTENTS

Contents

This chapter examines in much detail how the market mechanism operates. The chapter is divided into the following areas:

1 **Definitions** This topic has many words which, once again, we need to define quite precisely.
2 **Demand** Demand schedules, changes in demands, factors causing changes in demand, exceptional demand curves.
3 **Price elasticity of demand** The meaning of elasticity, measuring elasticity of demand, the importance of measuring elasticity of demand, influences on elasticity of demand.
4 **Income elasticity of demand.**
5 **Cross-price elasticity of demand.**
6 **Supply** Supply schedules, changes in supply, factors causing changes in supply.
7 **Price elasticity of supply** The meaning of elasticity of supply, measuring elasticity of supply, the importance of measuring elasticity of supply, influences on elasticity of supply.
8 **Equilibrium or market price.**
9 **The effects of changes in demand and supply on equilibrium.**

This topic involves a graphical and numerical analysis. It also involves the study of important concepts and ideas which are crucial to your understanding of Economics.

The workings of the market (or price) mechanism are the basis for the market economy system of allocating scarce resources discussed in Chapter 1. In the market economy scarce resources are allocated by private entrepreneurs. Price is the signal to the entrepreneur, and price is determined in the market by two opposing forces: supply and demand. Private entrepreneurs, motivated by maximizing profits, allocate scarce resources to the production of those commodities with rising prices.

1 DEFINITIONS

Before examining this mechanism of price determination, we should be aware of some important definitions:

(i) **Price** . . . the market value of goods and services bought by consumers. Price is measured in money units and is determined by the interplay of supply and demand.

(ii) **Value** . . . is not the same as price. The value given to a good or service will vary from consumer to consumer. Only *economic goods* have value (i.e. those goods and services which are limited in supply, which of course is the vast majority). *Free goods* have no value. Free goods are goods and services which are not limited in supply (fresh air).

(iii) **Demand** . . . the amount of a good or service which consumers are prepared to purchase at a given price and time. Demand is not the same as a want, e.g. I may want a Rolls-Royce car but unfortunately do not have sufficient money to demand it. Demand entails that a consumer is both willing and able to purchase a good or service.

(iv) **Supply** . . . the amount of a good or service which producers are prepared to offer for sale at a given price and time.

(v) **The market** . . . the opposing forces of supply and demand interact in the market to determine the price of a particular good or service. Demanders and suppliers are in contact with each other in the market. A market may actually be a building or location like the Stock Market (where the prices of securities are determined) or the Saturday morning fruit and vegetable market in your town. However, we could also refer to the British market for cars or washing machines, where there is no face-to-face contact between suppliers and demanders.

(vi) **Utility** . . . refers to the satisfaction consumers receive from consuming a good or service. Total utility is the total satisfaction gained from consuming all the potatoes an individual has consumed in a certain time period. Marginal utility is the satisfaction gained from consuming one more potato, which is the marginal unit (i.e. the one on the margin or last unit consumed). Clearly, to be consumed at all, a commodity must have utility. Marginal utility diminishes, however, with each unit of potatoes consumed.

2 DEMAND

(a) THE DEMAND SCHEDULE AND DEMAND CURVE

Each consumer will have his or her own demand schedule for a good or service. Normally, the higher the price of the commodity, the lower the demand; the lower the price of the commodity, higher the demand. It is possible to refer to a market (or composite) demand schedule for a commodity, which is each individual's demand schedule added together. Consider the market demand schedule for potatoes:

Price (pence per kg)	Quantity demanded (kg)
5	300
6	280
7	250
8	200
9	140
10	110

This information can be translated into graph form, and a demand curve can be illustrated. Note that we always plot price on the vertical axis and quantity on the horizontal axis. This being so, the demand curve slopes downwards from left to right, indicating that at high prices there is a low demand and at low prices there is a high demand.

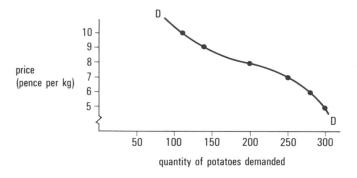

(b) CHANGES IN DEMAND

If the price of potatoes changes, consumers move along the demand curve. If price increases, consumers will consume less. There could, however, be a fundamental change in the demand for potatoes. For some reason, or reasons, all consumers are purchasing more (or fewer) potatoes at existing prices. Thus the whole demand curve for potatoes will shift to the right (or left).

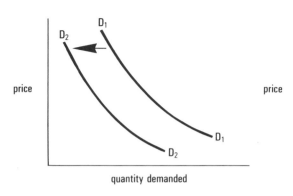

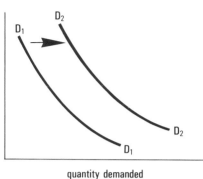

A decrease in demand at all prices. The demand curve has shifted to the left.

An increase in demand at all prices. The demand curve has shifted to the right.

| (c) FACTORS CAUSING CHANGES IN DEMAND | (i) Changes in consumer tastes. Potatoes may be more (or less) popular. |

(c) FACTORS CAUSING CHANGES IN DEMAND

(i)   Changes in consumer tastes. Potatoes may be more (or less) popular.

(ii)   Changes in the price of substitutes. A substitute good is something which can be used instead of potatoes. If rice (a potato substitute) increases in price, then more potatoes will be demanded (and vice versa).

(iii)   Changes in the price of complementaries. A complementary good is something which can be used with potatoes. If fish becomes very cheap, more consumers may have fish 'n' chips and demand for potatoes will increase (and vice versa).

(iv)   Changes in consumer incomes. If consumers are better off, they may purchase more potatoes.

(v)   Changes in the size of population. If there are more consumers, there will be an increase in demand for potatoes.

(vi)   Successful advertising by potato producers will increase demand for potatoes.

(d) EXCEPTIONAL DEMAND CURVES

A normal demand curve always slopes downwards from left to right. There are, however, rare instances of exceptional demand curves for goods known as Giffen goods. For instance, goods with snob appeal or goods being bought for speculative purposes (i.e. to make a profit) may have increased demand as price increases between certain price levels. Alternatively, a good which is regarded as inferior may suffer a drop in demand as the price drops. Consumers may prefer to purchase a slightly better-quality good with any savings made.

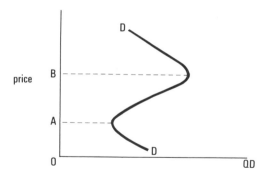

A good having snob appeal. Between price 0A and 0B demand actually increases.

3 PRICE ELASTICITY OF DEMAND

(a) THE MEANING OF PRICE ELASTICITY OF DEMAND

A price change can cause a big or small change in the demand for a commodity. If a change in price causes a much bigger change in demand, demand is elastic (i.e. responsive to price changes). If a change in price causes a smaller change in demand, demand is inelastic (i.e. not responsive to price changes). There are various categories of elasticity of demand:

(i) Perfectly inelastic demand Any change in price has no effect on demand.

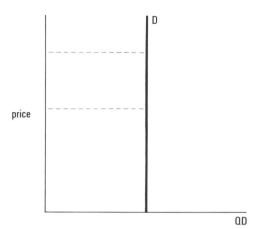

(ii)   **Inelastic demand** A change in price has little effect on demand.

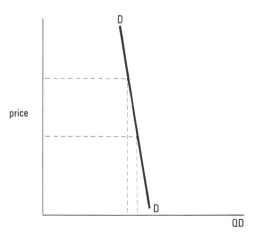

(iii)   **Unit elastic demand** A change in price has a proportionate (equal) effect on demand.

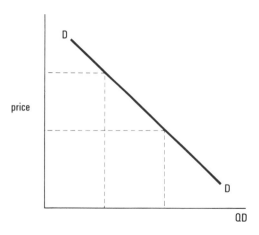

(iv)   **Elastic demand** A change in price has a great effect on demand.

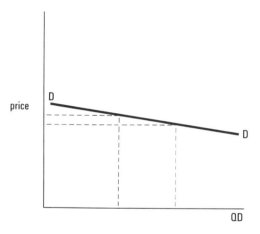

(v) Perfectly elastic demand Any change in price will have an infinite effect on demand.

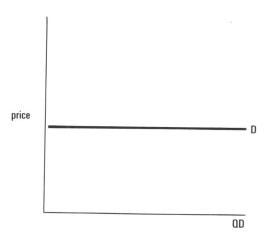

(b) MEASURING THE PRICE ELASTICITY OF DEMAND

Price elasticity of demand can be measured by the formula:

$$\frac{\text{proportionate (or percentage) change in demand}}{\text{proportionate (or percentage) change in price}}$$

If we refer to the demand schedule on p.31, a price rise from 5p to 6p causes demand to drop from 300kg to 280kg.

$$\text{Price elasticity of demand} = \frac{\frac{20}{3000}}{\frac{1}{5}} = \frac{\frac{1}{15}}{\frac{1}{5}} = \frac{1}{15} \times \frac{5}{1} = \frac{1}{3}$$

Alternatively, if price rises from 7p to 8p causes demand to drop from 250kg to 200kg:

$$\text{Price elasticity of demand} = \frac{\frac{50}{250}}{\frac{1}{7}} = \frac{\frac{1}{5}}{\frac{1}{7}} = \frac{1}{5} \times \frac{7}{1} = 1\frac{2}{5}$$

The numerical value of elasticity corresponds with one of the categories of elasticity of demand:

Numerical value	Category of elasticity of demand
Infinity	Perfectly elastic demand
1 $\longrightarrow$ Infinity	Elastic demand
1	Unit elastic demand
0 $\longrightarrow$ 1	Inelastic demand
0	Perfectly inelastic demand

(c) THE IMPORTANCE OF MEASURING ELASTICITY OF DEMAND

If a producer can calculate the price elasticity of demand for the commodity produced, the desirability (or not) of a price change can be determined. For instance, if one producer knows that demand between 5p and 6p is $\frac{1}{3}$, demand is inelastic. A price increase will cause demand to drop by a smaller proportion, and revenues (receipts) can be increased. However, if demand between 7p and 8p is $1\frac{3}{5}$, demand is elastic. A price increase will cause demand to drop by a larger proportion and revenues will be decreased.

A knowledge of elasticity is also valuable at budget time (see p.188) to the Chancellor of the Exchequer. The Chancellor will know that an increase in tax on commodities with inelastic demand will cause demand to drop by a smaller proportion and tax revenues can be increased.

(d) INFLUENCES ON ELASTICITY OF DEMAND

(i)   Necessities or luxuries . . . If a commodity is considered to be a necessity, demand will probably be inelastic because it is urgently required.

(ii)   Availability of substitute . . . If a commodity has many substitutes, demand will probably be elastic because alternatives can easily be found.

(iii)   Habit . . . If a commodity is habit-forming it will probably have inelastic demand because it is urgently required.

(iv)   The level of prices . . . A very cheap commodity will probably have inelastic demand because it does not account for much of an individual's expenditure.

4 INCOME ELASTICITY OF DEMAND

Demand also responds to changes in income as well as price. Income elasticity of demand is defined as:

$$\frac{\text{proportionate (or percentage) change in demand}}{\text{proportionate (or percentage) change in income}}$$

There are various categories of income elasticity of demand:

(i) Elastic . . . Demand changes by a greater proportion than income. The fraction will be greater than 1.

(ii) Unity . . . Demand changes by the same proportion as income. The fraction will be equal to 1.

(iii) Inelastic . . . Demand changes by a lesser proportion than income. The fraction will be less than 1.

(iv) Zero ... Demand does not change even if income changes. The numerical value will be zero.

(v) Negative ... Demand decreases as income increases. The numerical value will be negative.

An individual's income elasticity of demand for a particular commodity will depend to a great extent on his/her present standard of living. For instance, a very rich individual will probably have zero income elasticity for most commodities.

Income elasticity of demand is important to manufacturers because they can calculate future production levels from anticipated income changes amongst consumers. They can plan to meet the increase in demand.

5 CROSS-PRICE ELASTICITY OF DEMAND

Demand for some commodities can be affected by changes in the price of others. Cross-price elasticity of demand is measured by the formula:

$$\frac{\text{proportionate (or percentage) change in demand for good A}}{\text{proportionate (or percentage) change in the price of good B}}$$

If goods A and B are complements, the answer will be negative (−) because if good B increases in price, the demand for good A will decline. A large negative answer indicates close complements.

If goods A and B are substitutes, the answer will be positive (+) because if good B increases in price, the demand for good A will increase. A large positive answer indicates close substitutes.

Now answer the following multiple-choice questions:

MC1 The diagram below shows an increase in the demand for beef.

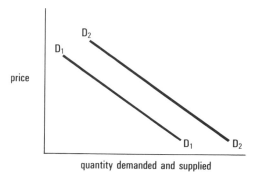

This change could be explained by:

(a)   successful advertising by beef producers

(b)   decrease in the price of pork
(c)   more efficient farming methods being used by beef producers
(d)   an increase in wages paid to beef farm workers
(e)   people eating less of all types of meat

MC2   Which of the following products have a complementary demand?
(a)   pork and beef
(b)   motorbikes and cars
(c)   tennis rackets and tennis balls
(d)   crude oil and petrol
(e)   bananas and apples

MC3   Income elasticity of demand is calculated by the formula:

(a) $\dfrac{\text{percentage change in income}}{\text{percentage change in quantity demanded}}$

(b) $\dfrac{\text{percentage change in price}}{\text{percentage change in quantity demanded}}$

(c) $\dfrac{\text{percentage change in income}}{\text{percentage change in price}}$

(d) $\dfrac{\text{percentage change in quantity demanded}}{\text{percentage change in price}}$

(e) $\dfrac{\text{percentage change in quantity demanded}}{\text{percentage change in income}}$

MC4   A company manufacturing radios found that when it lowered its selling price from £30 to £20 per unit, the number of radios sold per month increased from 100,000 to 140,000. The price elasticity of demand for the company's radios was therefore:

(a) $\frac{2}{5}$
(b) $\frac{5}{6}$
(c)   1
(d) $1\frac{1}{5}$
(e) $1\frac{1}{2}$

Multiple-choice questions **MC5** and **MC6** are based on the table below, which gives information about the demand for apples and pears:

Apples

Price (pence per lb)		Quantity demanded per week (lbs)
Week 1	20	250
Week 2	15	300

Pears

Price (pence per lb)		Quantity demanded per week (lbs)
Week 1	20	200
Week 2	20	100

MC5   The cross-elasticity of demand between apples and pears if the price of apples falls from 20p to 15p is:

(a) $\frac{1}{2}$
(b)   1
(c) $1\frac{1}{2}$
(d)   2
(e) $2\frac{1}{2}$

MC6   The price-elasticity of demand for apples if the price falls from 20p to 15p is:

(a) $\frac{2}{5}$
(b) $\frac{4}{5}$
(c)   1
(d) $1\frac{2}{5}$
(e) $1\frac{4}{5}$

6 SUPPLY

(a) THE SUPPLY SCHEDULE AND SUPPLY CURVE

Suppliers are motivated by profit. If prices are high they expect to make more profit and therefore supply more. Consider the market supply schedule for potatoes:

Price (pence per lb)	Quantity supplied (kg)
5	75
6	120
7	170
8	200
9	240
10	280

This information can be translated into graph form and a supply curve can be illustrated. This being so, one supply curve slopes upwards from left to right, indicating that at high prices there is a high supply and at low prices there is a low supply.

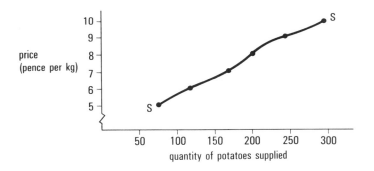

(b) CHANGES IN SUPPLY   If the price of potatoes changes, suppliers move along the supply curve. If price increases, suppliers supply more. There could, however, be a fundamental change in the supply of potatoes. For some reason, or reasons, all supplies are supplying more (or fewer) potatoes at existing prices. Thus the whole supply curve for potatoes will shift to the right (or left):

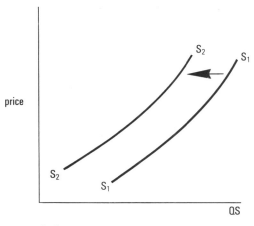

A decrease in supply at all
prices. The supply curve has
shifted to the left.

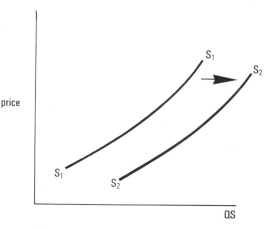

An increase in supply at all
prices. The supply curve has
shifted to the right.

**(c) FACTORS CAUSING
CHANGES IN SUPPLY**

(i)   Changes in climate. This would especially affect agricultural
products such as potatoes.

(ii)   Technical changes. New developments (better types of
potatoes) may increase the supply of potatoes.

(ii)   Changes in the cost of producing potatoes:

– if potato workers received higher wages or if the price of
equipment increased, supply might decrease.

– a tax on potato producers may cause them to reduce their
production of potatoes.

– a subsidy to potato producers may cause them to increase
the production of potatoes.

7 PRICE ELASTICITY OF SUPPLY

**(a) THE MEANING OF
ELASTICITY OF SUPPLY**

We have already observed that as price increases, supply will also
increase. However, supply may change by more than price (elastic
supply) or by less than price (inelastic supply). Elasticity of supply
shows by how much supply alters in response to a change in price.

There are various categories of elasticity of supply:

(i) **Perfectly inelastic supply** Any change in price has no effect on supply

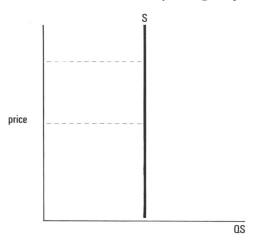

(ii) **Inelastic supply** A change in price has little effect on supply.

(iii) Unit elastic supply A change in price has a proportionate (equal) effect on supply.

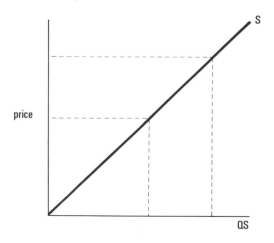

(iv) Elastic supply A change in price has a great effect on supply.

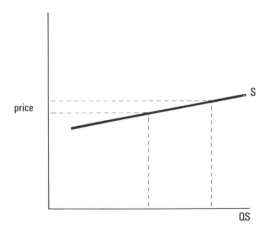

(v) Perfectly elastic supply Any change in price will have an infinite effect on supply.

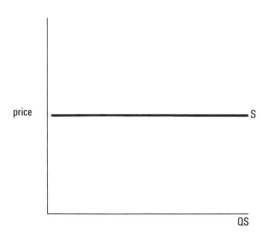

(b) MEASURING THE PRICE OF SUPPLY

Price elasticity of supply can be measured by the formula:

$$\frac{\text{proportionate (or percentage) change in supply}}{\text{proportionate (or percentage) change in price}}$$

If we refer to one supply schedule on p.40, a price rise from 8p to 9p causes supply to increase from 200kg to 240kg.

$$\text{Price elasticity of supply} = \frac{\frac{40}{200}}{\frac{1}{8}} = \frac{\frac{1}{5}}{\frac{1}{8}} = \frac{1}{5} \times \frac{8}{1} = 1\frac{3}{5}$$

The numerical value of elasticity corresponds with one of the categories of elasticity of supply:

Numerical value	Category of elasticity of supply
Infinity	Perfectly elastic supply
1 $\longrightarrow$ Infinity	Elastic supply
1	Unit elastic supply
0 $\longrightarrow$ 1	Inelastic supply
0	Perfectly inelastic supply

(c) THE IMPORTANCE OF MEASURING ELASTICITY OF SUPPLY

Producers need to know the elasticity of supply of their commodity so that they know if they can respond quickly to any change in price (and demand).

(d) INFLUENCES ON ELASTICITY OF SUPPLY

(i)   Availability of stocks ... If stocks of the commodity can be kept kept, supply can easily be expanded and supply is relatively elastic.

(ii)   Spare capacity ... If there is a great deal of spare labour and machinery in the industry, the producer will be able to expand supply fairly easily and supply is relatively elastic.

(iii)   Attracting factors of production ... If extra land, labour, capital and enterprise can easily be attracted into the industry, the producer will be able to expand supply fairly easily and supply will again be relatively elastic.

(iv)   The time period ... In the short run, supply tends to be rather more inelastic than in the long run. Indeed, in the momentary (i.e. immediate) period, supply may be perfectly inelastic. The longer the time period, the more elastic will be supply.

Answer the following multiple-choice question:

MC7   The diagrams below show five possible supply curves.

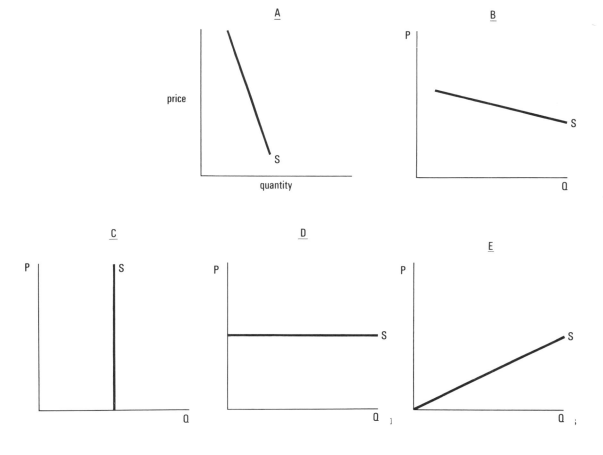

Which of these curves would most likely represent the supply conditions for tickets for a pop concert to be held at Wembley Stadium?

8 EQUILIBRIUM (OR MARKET) PRICE

The equilibrium price is determined by the opposing forces, demand and supply. Equilibrium means balance. Thus equilibrium price is where the market is in balance – it is where demand equals supply. So, equilibrium price is the market price.

Let us consider the demand and supply schedules for potatoes again:

Price (pence per kg)	Supply (kg)	Demand (kg)
5	75	300
6	120	280
7	170	250
8	200	200
9	240	140
10	280	110

We can translate this information into graph form:

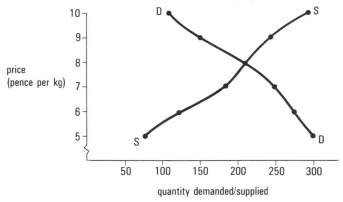

From both the schedule and the graph we can see that demand equals supply at 8p per kg and the quantity demanded and supplied is 200kg.

If suppliers tried to force prices above 8p per kg there would be a glut of potatoes and prices would have to fall back to equilibrium price 8p per kg. On the other hand, if suppliers (mistakenly) set the price below 8p per kg there would be a shortage of potatoes and prices would rise to equilibrium price 8p per kg. The market will have to settle at equilibrium or market price.

9 THE EFFECTS OF CHANGES IN DEMAND AND SUPPLY ON EQUILIBRIUM

(a) AN INCREASE IN DEMAND FOR POTATOES

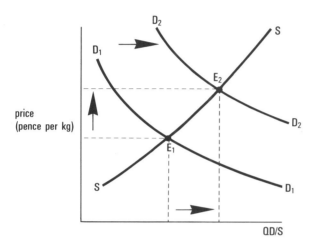

If the demand for potatoes increases, the demand curve shifts from D^1 to D^2 and equilibrium is now at E^2. Equilibrium price has risen; so has output.

(b) A DECREASE IN DEMAND FOR POTATOES

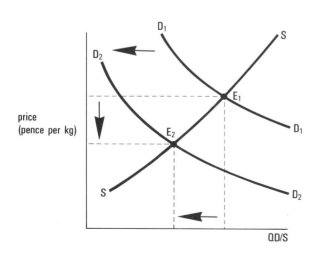

If the demand for potatoes decreases, the demand curve shifts from D^1 to D^2 and equilibrium is now at E^2. Equilibrium price has fallen; so has output.

(c) AN INCREASE IN SUPPLY OF POTATOES

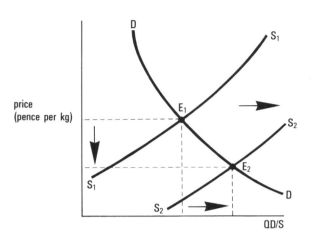

If the supply of potatoes increases, the supply curve shifts from S^1 to S^2 and equilibrium is now at E^2. Equilibrium price has fallen, but output has increased.

(d) A DECREASE IN SUPPLY OF POTATOTES

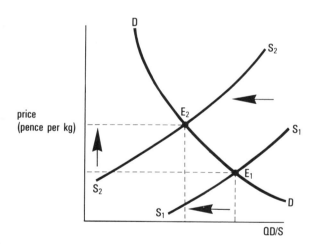

If the supply of potatoes decreases, supply curve shifts from S^1 to S^2 and equilibrium is now at E^2. Equilibrium price has risen, and output has decreased.

Answer the following multiple-choice question:

Multiple-choice questions MC8 and MC9 are based on the graph at top of next page, which shows the market for apples:

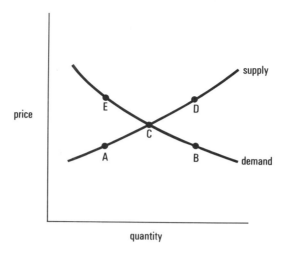

quantity

MC8 Which one of the positions A, B, C, D, or E could become the equilibrium position in the market if bad weather results in low crop yields?

MC9 Which one of the positions A, B, C, D, or E could become the equilibrium position in the market if there is a medical report stating that eating apples prevents illness?

MC10 The following diagram refers to the market equilibrium for petrol:

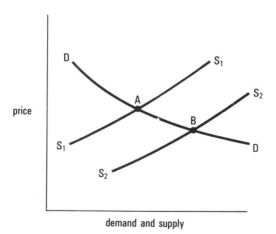

demand and supply

A shift of equilibrium from A to B reflects:
(*a*)   an increase in demand for petrol
(*b*)   more efficient methods of oil refining
(*c*)   fewer cars sold
(*d*)   an increase in tax on oil companies
(*e*)   a war between two major oil producers

1   With the aid of diagrams, explain:
     (*a*)   What is meant by equilibrium price?
     (*b*)   How will the following affect the equilibrium price of petrol in the UK market?
             (i) an increase in the price of cars
             (ii) the imposition of an export quota by oil-producing countries
             (iii) a subsidy paid by oil companies to petrol filling station chains.

2   (*a*)   What is meant by a market?
     (*b*)   With the aid of diagrams, distinguish between
             (i) an extension of demand
             (ii) an increase in demand.
     (*c*)   What factors might lead to an increase in demand for cars?
     (*d*)   With the aid of a diagram, show how an increase in car tax will affect the price of cars.

3   (*a*)   How does the price mechanism operate?
     (*b*)   How is the operation of market forces affected by the use of
             (i) expenditure taxes, and
             (ii) subsidies?
     (*c*)   Explain why the demand for rail transport might change.

4   (*a*)   What is meant by price elasticity of demand?
     (*b*)   What factors influence the price elasticity of demand?
     (*c*)   Why might the imposition of a further tax on beer reduce the revenue the government obtains from duty on beer?
     (*d*)   Why is the demand for cigarettes relatively inelastic?

5   (*a*)   Define elasticity of supply.
     (*b*)   Discuss the significance of elasticity of supply and how it might be measured.
     (*c*)   What factors govern the elasticity of supply for fresh flowers?

DATA RESPONSE

A bus company provides a regular daily service between a small village and a large town. The market demand for return tickets varies according to the fares shown below:

Demand for return tickets per week	Fare for the return journey (pence)
3,000	4
2,500	5
2,000	6
1,500	7
1,000	8
500	9

At present the bus company charges 6p per return journey and sells 2,000 return tickets per week. Answer all the questions below.

(*a*)   What is the company's total revenue per week?

(*b*)   At what level of demand does the bus company maximize total revenue?

(*c*)   Showing all your workings, calculate the price elasticity of demand for a rise in fares from 6p to 8p.

(*d*)   Describe the effects of a sudden rise in fares on
  (i) the community
  (ii) the demand for other forms of transport
  (iii) the bus company.

Answers to multiple-choice questions:

MC1	(*a*)	MC6	(*b*)
MC2	(*c*)	MC7	(*c*)
MC3	(*e*)	MC8	(*e*)
MC4	(*d*)	MC9	(*d*)
MC5	(*d*)	MC10	(*b*)

PRODUCTION

CONTENTS

The chapter on Production covers the following topics:

1 **Types of production** Primary, secondary and tertiary production. The growth of tertiary production.
2 **Division of labour and specialization** Meaning, advantages, disadvantages, division of labour requires exchange, limitations, mass production.
3 **The law of eventually diminishing returns.**
4 **The costs of production** Fixed costs, variable costs, total costs, average costs, marginal costs, social costs.
5 **The location of industry** Factors influencing the location of industry, the assisted areas, regional policy.

1 TYPES OF PRODUCTION

Production is the creation of goods and services which consumers are prepared to purchase in order to satisfy human wants. Production is not finished until the good or service is in the hands of the final consumer. There are, broadly speaking, three categories of activities involved in the process of production:

(i)   primary production
(ii)   secondary production
(iii) tertiary production.

(i) Primary production . . . the first stage in the production process. It includes all those industries engaged in extracting raw materials, farming, forestry and fishing. The products of these industries are used by industries involved in secondary production.

(ii) Secondary production . . . includes all those industries involved in manufacturing the finished goods using the raw materials provided by primary industries. Examples include steel, brewing, car manufacture.

(iii) Tertiary production . . . industries involved in tertiary production do not produce goods at all. They provide the services which are necessary for the production to take place. There are two types of service:
–   personal services, such as doctors, dentists, and teachers, involved in providing a service to persons.
–   commercial services, which includes all those activities engaged in providing a service to industry such as banking, account-

ancy and advertising. They ensure that the finished good reaches the consumer at the right time, in the right place and in the right quantity and quality.

The growth of tertiary production in the modern developed economy

% shares of UK's GDP (total domestic output)

	1974	1979	1984
Primary industry	7.2	10.2	13.5
Secondary industry	37.9	34.7	29.9
Tertiary industry	54.9	55.1	56.6

Before the Industrial Revolution in Britain, the largest sector of production was agriculture. However, as Britain became more industrialized secondary production became the biggest sector, with industries such as steel, textiles and shipbuilding dominating economic activity. In Britain today tertiary production is the largest sector. There are several reasons for this state of affairs:
–   Agriculture, traditionally the largest primary industry, has become much more mechanized. This has had two effects. Firstly, less need to employ labour; second, increased efficiency and production.
–   Secondary industries have similarly become more mechanized and efficient. Such industries therefore require less labour but need more services to help in the distribution of the commodity.
–   The incomes and living standards of the British people have improved. When people become richer they demand proportionately more services.
–   The increasing social and economic role of successive governments has required a large civil service, more doctors and teachers.
This is a familiar pattern as an economy becomes wealthier. The transition goes from being a primary producer to a secondary producer and, finally, a tertiary producer. There are, of course, exceptions. Saudi Arabia and New Zealand, for instance, are both in some respects wealthy countries. The former's wealth is based on oil extraction and the latter's on agriculture. However, most primary-producing countries remain poor.
Note: primary industry has increase its share of UK national output since the early 1970s because of the development of North Sea oil.

MC1 Which one of the following is classed by economists as a tertiary industry?
(*a*)   farming

(b)   baking bread
(c)   banking
(d)   oil refining
(e)   fishing

MC2 Which of the following contains examples of both primary and secondary industries?
(a)   the sale of beer brewed on the premises
(b)   the manufacture and sale of video equipment
(c)   the building of a factory which is then used to manufacture washing machines
(d)   the growing of timber which is then used to manufacture paper
(e)   the drilling for oil and its sale to the public

2 THE DIVISION OF LABOUR AND SPECIALIZATION

(a) THE MEANING OF DIVISION OF LABOUR

In the modern economy factors of production tend to specialize in certain types of production. Labour tends to specialize – some people become teachers, others policemen, some become lawyers, and so on. Land tends to be put the specialist use – growing wheat, dairying or beef cattle. Capital and enterprise are likewise specialized. This is called the division of labour.

In the context of labour, division of labour occurs when the production process is divided up so that an individual undertakes only a small part of the total work. Division of labour was first supported by an early economist named Adam Smith, who in 1776 wrote a famous economics book entitled *The Wealth of Nations*. Smith used the production of pins as an example of how a firm's output could be expanded by employment of division of labour rather than each worker producing each pin. Most modern production lines (cars, washing machines, steel, etc.) use division of labour techniques.

(b) ADVANTAGES OF DIVISION OF LABOUR

The main advantage is that production is increased and the costs per unit of output are reduced because:
(i)   Time is saved because workers spend less time being trained and between jobs.
(ii)   There is more economic use of tools and machinery, because fewer tools will be needed and they will be in constant use.
(iii)   Workers develop skills doing repetitive tasks. Practice makes perfect.
(iv)   Workers can specialize in a job in which they have some ability.
(v)   Machinery can be developed to replace that labour doing the most basic repetitive tasks.

(c) DISADVANTAGES OF DIVISION OF LABOUR

(i)   Repetitive tasks are boring; this leads to absenteeism and industrial unrest amongst workers.

(ii)   Workers become alienated from fellow-workers and managers. They feel ignored and unimportant.

(iii)   Workers become little more than machine-minders and there is a loss of traditional skills.

(iv)   All workers are interdependent and if disruption occurs in one part of the production process, then the whole process may be brought to a halt.

(v)   There is a lack of variety in the commodities which are produced.

(vi)   Some occupations involve the possibility of danger or disease, e.g. soldiers may be killed in action.

(d) DIVISION OF LABOUR REQUIRES EXCHANGE

In an economy adopting division of labour techniques there must be exchange. The farmer must exchange food for the tailor's clothes, and vice versa. In a modern economy the exchange of goods for goods (known as barter) would obviously be awkward and cumbersome. Thus the efficient exchange of goods and services is helped by a well-developed money and banking system. Money acts as a medium of exchange. Also, a sophisticated transport system allows commodities to be distributed from producers to consumers quickly and efficiently.

(e) DIVISION OF LABOUR IS LIMITED BY THE SIZE OF THE MARKET

If division of labour is to be employed successfully, there must be an adequate demand for the commodity which has been produced in greater quantities. It would not be worth while to produce many units of commodity X if only a few people consume it.

(f) MASS PRODUCTION

Division of labour techniques developed in the twentieth century into mass production. This is a system of production aimed at the highest output with the fewest workers, by means of simplification and standardization of the commodities being produced. Mass production is clearly to be seen in car factories, where work flows continuously through the factory with workers performing their tasks as each unit passes by.

MC3   Which of the following is *not* an advantage of division of labour?
(*a*)   workers become dependent on other workers
(*b*)   workers are trained more easily
(*c*)   workers spend less time moving from job to job

(d)   workers become more efficient at performing repetitive jobs
(e)   machinery is more easily introduced to perform simple tasks

MC4   As the division of labour increases in an economy:
(a)   a greater percentage of the working population is employed in primary industries
(b)   interdependence between people and firms diminishes.
(c)   the standard of living of workers falls
(d)   the proportion of specialists in the labour force declines
(e)   the proportion of workers employed in tertiary production rises

MC5   The employment of workers in specialist occupations is called
(a)   a subsistence economy
(b)   mobility of labour
(c)   skilled labour
(d)   division of labour
(e)   automation

3 THE LAW OF EVENTUALLY DIMINISHING RETURNS

It would seem that production can be continuously increased by combining more and more factors of production. However, the law of (eventually) diminishing returns shows that this does not happen. Also, after a certain level of production the costs of production begin to rise.

The law of diminishing returns states that as successive units of variable factors of production (i.e. those which can be changed in supply, such as labour) are added to a unit of fixed factor of production (i.e. that which cannot be changed in supply, such as land), additions to production will increase, reach a maximum and then diminish.

The law can be illustrated by the following table:

Land	Units of labour	Total output	Extra output (called marginal output)	Average output
1	1	10	10	10
1	2	21	11	10.5
1	3	33	12	11
1	4	46	13	11.5
1	5	60	14	12
1	6	73	13	12.1
1	7	83	10	11.8

Land	Units of labour	Total output	Extra output (called marginal output)	Average output
1	8	91	8	11.3
1	9	96	5	10.7

Note: Marginal output (product) is the addition to total output caused by adding one more unit of variable factor (labour).

    Average output (product)) is total output divided by the number of units of variable factor.

We can see from the marginal output column that the second labourer added more to output than did the first, the third labourer added more than the second, and so on. Thus returns are increasing. After the fifth labourer, however, additions to output begin to diminish. If we carried on, even total output would begin to diminish.

The law of diminishing returns helps to explain how costs of production rise as we combine more and more factors of production.

4 THE COSTS OF PRODUCTION

The costs of production are the money expenditures on the use of factors of production by the firm. There are several different types of costs which can be identified:

(i) **Fixed costs** . . . do not change with output (at least in the short period). Fixed costs include interest repayments, rents, rates and salaries.

(ii) **Variable costs** . . . do change with output. As output increases, variable costs also increase. Variable costs include wages and raw materials. If a firm wishes to remain in business then it must, in the short period, cover variable costs with revenues (or receipts). If it does not do this, the firm would be better off leaving the industry.

(iii) **Total costs** . . . are fixed and variable costs added together. Total costs will increase as output increases. If a firm wishes to remain in business in the long run, it must cover total costs with revenues (or receipts).

(iv) **Average costs** . . . are total costs divided by the number of units produced. The law of diminishing returns explains average costs. If in the table all labourers received an equal wage, the average costs would fall, reach a minimum and then increase. When costs per unit are at a minimum, this is called the *optimum* level of output.

(v) **Marginal cost** . . . is the cost of producing one extra unit, called the marginal unit. The law of diminishing returns also explains marginal costs. If in the table all labourers received an equal wage, the marginal costs would fall, reach a minimum and then increase.

Average cost and marginal cost curves

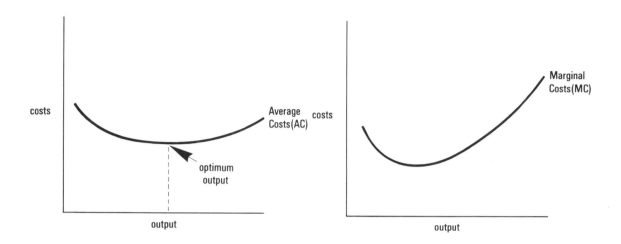

Marginal costs are very important, because the level of output where marginal costs are equal to marginal revenue (the revenue gained from the extra unit produced) will be the most profitable level of output. This is called *equilibrium* output.

(vi) Social costs ... are the costs to the community as a whole of producing particular goods. It is an attempt to measure the deaths of labourers, pollution and environmental damage. For instance, the mining of coal may lead to spoil heaps and deaths of miners. Both the production and consumption of commodities may involve social costs and social benefits (called externalities). These social costs and benefits are usually ignored by private entrepreneurs, who are concerned only with money costs and benefits. Nevertheless, increasingly in both public and private enterprise a technique known as *cost-benefit analysis* is being used to measure social costs and benefits. A main problem, however, is the measurement of social costs and benefits, e.g. how is death valued?

MC6 Increased pollution resulting from the building of a factory is an example of
(*a*)   marginal costs
(*b*)   social costs
(*c*)   fixed costs
(*d*)   opportunity costs
(*e*)   total costs

MC7 The following table refers to the total cost of producing different numbers of radios:

Output	Total cost (£)
1	50
2	100
3	130
4	170
5	220

The radio with the marginal cost of £40 is the
(a)   first
(b)   second
(c)   third
(d)   fourth
(e)   fifth

MC8 The following table shows the costs of production at a firm's various outputs:

Units produced	Total costs
0	50
1	90
2	120
3	135
4	140
5	150

When the average total cost was £30, the variable costs were:
(a)   £60
(b)   £70
(c)   £80
(d)   £90
(e)   £100

5 THE LOCATION OF INDUSTRY: REGIONAL SPECIALIZATION

Another type of specialization (discussed on pp.57–9 in relation to specialization by individuals) is regional specialization. This is the tendency of certain industries to be located in certain regions. There are many examples in the UK such as the car industry in the West Midlands, textiles in Lancashire and Yorkshire and pottery in the Potteries (i.e. Stoke-on-Trent).

(a) FACTORS INFLUENCING THE LOCATION OF INDUSTRY

Firms will locate where costs of production per unit of output are at their lowest and where the firm is, as a result, more profitable. There are several factors which the firm will take in account:

(i) TRANSPORT COSTS

The firm will want to locate itself where transport costs are at their lowest. Much will depend on the situation of the *market* and *raw materials*. Firms will not want to be too far away from either their raw materials or their market. There could, however, be a problem when the raw material is in one area and the market in another.

Material-orientated industries . . . If the raw material is more expensive to transport than the finished commodity, the firm will locate nearer to the raw materials (e.g. steel).

Market-orientated industries . . . If the finished commodity is more expensive to transport than the raw material, the firm will locate nearer to the market (e.g. motor vehicles).

Some industries can be located near to either the market or the raw material. These are termed 'foot loose' industries.

(ii) POWER SUPPLIES

Firms need power to provide heat and light and to drive machinery. Before the development of the national grid system, being near a coal field was very important because coal provided power. This is why many old and traditional industries are located in the coal-field areas of the UK, such as South Wales and Central Scotland. With the development of the national grid, firms can be located anywhere in the UK and yet still receive power.

(iii) NEARNESS TO FACTORS OF PRODUCTION

Firms will require land, labour, capital and enterprise in the correct quantity and quality.

(iv) THE EXTERNAL ECONOMIES OF SCALE

The external economies of scale are those advantages which apply to all firms in the industry as a result of being located in a particular area. The other category of economies of scale is the internal economies of scale discussed on pp.76–7.

The external economies of scale are developed over a period of time in a particular region. All firms can enjoy them, but large firms can take advantage of these economies to a proportionately greater extent. Here are some external economies of scale:

A pool of skilled labour will develop in a particular area. For instance, many workers in the Stoke-on-Trent area are skilled at pottery work.

Subsidiary or ancillary firms develop which provide the main industry with components. For instance, in the West Midlands there are many car component firms.

Local services and education facilities will develop, dominated by the needs of the main industry in the area.

Transport and communications systems develop, to the advantage of all firms in the area.

(v) INERTIA

This happens when a certain area becomes traditionally famous for producing a certain commodity. This tradition will be a factor for the firm to take into account when choosing where to locate.

(vi) SPECIAL FACTORS

There may be special influences on location for certain industries:

Climate This was important in determining the location of textiles in Lancashire and Yorkshire. Cotton needed a damp environment. It is also important in determining the location of agricultural activities.

Plenty of cheap flat land is important in locating oil refineries.

Safety factors: nuclear power stations need to be located away from major population areas.

Personal factors: the entrepreneur may have a personal preference for a certain part of the country. It may be that the entrepreneur (like Lord Nuffield, who as William Morris developed Morris motorcars in Oxford) will locate the firm in his/her home town.

(vii) GOVERNMENT REGIONAL POLICY

The government has developed a regional policy to help depressed areas like Scotland, Northern Ireland, Wales and Northern England.

These areas are called assisted areas. Regional policy is discussed in the next section.

(b) THE ASSISTED AREAS

Regional policy is an attempt by government to overcome the economic problems – notably unemployment – of the assisted areas.

(i) WHERE ARE THE ASSISTED AREAS?

The government differentiates between two types of assisted area: intermediate areas and development areas.

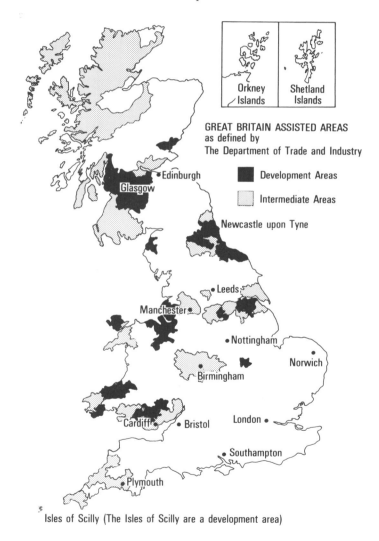

Isles of Scilly (The Isles of Scilly are a development area)

More recently the government has identified a number of *enterprise zones* which are derelict areas lacking in industrial development, mainly to be found in inner cities. Firms in these zones receive a range of government aid such as simplified planning procedures for further building, tax allowances and grants for firms.

(ii) WHY ARE THERE ASSISTED AREAS?

The assisted areas overspecialized in one industry (or in some cases a few) which is now in decline. South Wales concentrated on coal and steel, both of which are in decline because of competition from other countries and from new products. Similarly, the North of England concentrated on textiles, Tyneside and Clydeside on shipbuilding. Because these old traditional (or staple) industries of coal, shipbuilding, steel and textiles are now in decline, so too are the regions which they formerly dominated. This has led to the existence of structural unemployment (see pp.171–2) in the assisted regions.

(iii) WHAT ARE THE PROBLEMS TO BE FOUND IN THE ASSISTED AREAS?

All the assisted areas have certain common characteristics. The main problem is high unemployment, above the UK natural average. Other problems include a poor regional capital infrastructure (i.e. roads, hospitals, schools, etc.); lower income per head than the national average; an ageing population as young people leave to find work elsewhere; lower levels of educational achievement and a higher level of social problems.

(iv) GOVERNMENT CONCERN ABOUT ASSISTED AREAS

The government is concerned to do something for the assisted areas, not least because there is a waste of scarce factors of production (resources are unemployed) and because of the financial costs of supporting unemployed labour. Of course, there is also a social (as opposed to economic) argument in favour of helping the assisted areas to alleviate the misery and unhappiness which unemployment brings to the worker and his/her family.

(c) GOVERNMENT REGIONAL POLICY

Government regional policy is based on the Industrial Development Act 1984.

Regional policy is an attempt by government to persuade firms to move to the assisted areas, thereby creating jobs and incomes in those areas. This policy is called 'taking the work to the workers'. The policy consists of two different approaches. Firstly, financial inducements to firms to move into the dpressed areas, such as loans, grants, payments of removal expenses, advance factories, factories built and provided rent-free and retraining of workers. The main form of assistance is the regional development grant, which is available only to those firms operating within development areas. The regional development grant is calculated either by 15 per cent of qualifying project cost or £10,000 for each new job created by the project (if the firm already employs more than 200 people). Secondly, measures to persuade firms to move out of so-called growth areas (i.e. more prosperous areas in the South and South-East of England), such as refusal to allow development of buildings.

The government itself has set an example to private industry by moving many of its departments out to the assisted areas – the Royal Mint to Llantrisant (South Wales) and National Giro to Bootle (Merseyside). The government has also built new towns, such as Milton Keynes and Telford, to attract firms out of the large urban areas.

Since joining the European Community in 1973, Britain can also call on resources from the Community's regional fund, set up to help regionally depressed areas throughout the community.

MC9   Where bulk is decreased during the production of a good, a firm is likely to produce near to
(a)   its source of power
(b)   its source of raw materials
(c)   its market
(d)   good motorways
(e)   component firms

MC10   Which of the following characteristics is common to all the development areas?
(a)   levels of unemployment above the national average
(b)   poor transport facilities
(c)   low levels of population
(d)   too much dependence on textiles
(e)   too much dependence on primary industries

EXTENDED WRITING QUESTIONS

1   (a)   Using modern examples, explain the meaning of 'division of labour'.
(b)   What is meant by the statement 'specialization is limited by the extent of the market'?
(c)   What are the advantages and disadvantages of division of labour?
(d)   Explain the meaning of mass production.

2   (a)   Distinguish between primary and secondary production.
(b)   Explain the meaning of tertiary production, giving appropriate examples.
(c)   Why may this branch of production be considered as essential as the primary and secondary industries?

(*d*)   What are the likely consequences of an expanding tertiary sector?

3 (*a*)   Distinguish between tertiary, secondary and primary production.
(*b*)   As an economy develops, what changes usually occur in the relative importance of these forms of production?
(*c*)   Explain the recent relative increase in primary production in the UK.
(*d*)   Why is tertiary production now the largest sector in the UK economy?

4 (*a*)   Select two major industries.
         (i) State their locations.
         (ii) Compare the factors determining their location.
(*b*)   (i) Why and
         (ii) how does the government attempt to influence the location of industry?
(*c*)   How successful has regional policy been?

5 (*a*)   What is the regional problem?
(*b*)   Briefly explain the different types of assistance available to firms which locate in an assisted area.
(*c*)   What are the disadvantages of UK regional policy?
(*d*)   What factors should a firm take into consideration when deciding whether to build a new factory in a development area?

DATA RESPONSE   1   The table below to changes in the percentage level of regional unemployment in 1982 and 1985.

Region	1982 % unemployed	1985 % unemployed
United Kingdom	12.1	13.5
South-East	8.5	9.9
East Anglia	9.7	10.7
East Midlands	11.0	12.7
West Midlands	14.7	15.5
Yorkshire and Humberside	13.2	15.1
South West	10.6	12.0
North West	14.7	16.3
Wales	15.4	16.9
Scotland	14.0	15.6
North	16.6	18.9
Northern Ireland	18.7	21.0

Source: *Department of Employment Gazette*

(*a*)   Define unemployment.
(*b*)   Describe three types of unemployment which may exist in an economy.

(c)   (i) Which region had the highest unemployment rate in 1985?
         (ii) Which region had the lowest unemployment rate in 1985?
(d)   How do you account for these regional variations in unemployment?
(e)   Briefly explain the different types of assistance now available to firms which locate in assisted areas.

Answer

(a)   Unemployment is now officially defined as the problem of all those people who are registered as unemployed and in receipt of unemployment benefits. See pp.170–1 for detailed definition and criticisms of this definition.

(b)   Choose any three from the various types of unemployment, discussed on pp.171–2.

(c)   (i) Northern Ireland, with 21 per cent of the labour force registered as unemployed.
         (ii) South-East England, with 9.9 per cent of the labour force registered as unemployed.

(d)   Some regions have unemployment rates above the national average mainly because of structural unemployment, which has developed into regional unemployment. These regions were dominated by a few industries now in decline because of foreign competition (at home and abroad) and technological innovations. There are few alternative sources of employment in these areas. The problem is compounded by geographical and occupational immobility of labour (see pp.122–3). Refer to specific regions and their particular problems, e.g. the decline of the car industry in the West Midlands.

Other regions have suffered less because the newer and more technologically based industries are expanding in these regions (e.g. the South-East of England. These areas are more populated (larger market) and nearer to the UK's main markets (i.e. the European Community).

(e)   You need to discuss the various types of aid available to the assisted areas. Make special reference to the enterprise zones.

The main method of regional aid is the regional development grant. Also include other grants, allowances and help, such as advance factories. Differentiate between development areas and intermediate areas – more help is available to development areas.

2   Study the various illustrations which are labelled A to F.

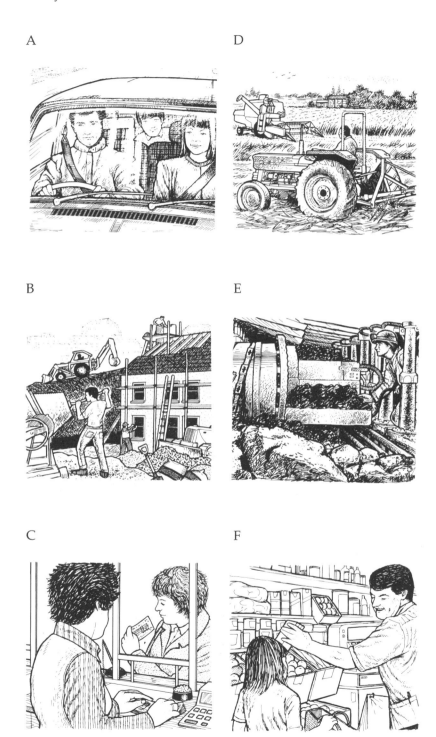

A

B

C

D

E

F

(a)   Distinguish between:
    (i) a good and a service – give one example of each from the illustrations.
    (ii) a capital good and a consumer good – give one example of each from the illustrations.

(b)   Classify into primary production, secondary production and tertiary production the people working in
    (i) illustration B
    (ii) illustration D
    (iii) illustration F.

Study the pie charts below, then answer questions (c) to (e).

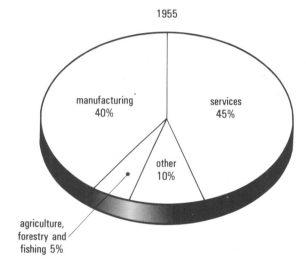

1955

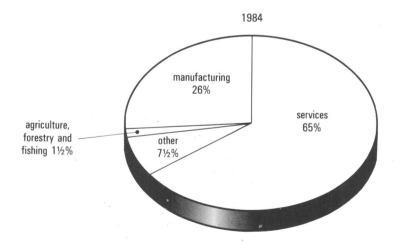

1984

The changing distribution of employment in the UK

(c)   Describe the changes which have taken place in the distribution of employment in the UK between 1955 and 1984.

(d)   Give reasons for these changes.

(e)   Examine the likely economic effects of these changes.

Answers to multiple-choice questions:

MC1	(c)		**MC6**	(b)
MC2	(d)		**MC7**	(d)
MC3	(a)		**MC8**	(e)
MC4	(e)		**MC9**	(b)
MC5	(d)		**MC10**	(a)

THE SIZE OF FIRMS

CONTENTS

In this chapter we examine the size of firms. The chapter is subdivided as follows:

1   **The economies of large-scale production.** The increasing size of firms. The internal economies of scale such as technical economies, financial economies, commercial economies, managerial economies, research economies, welfare economies and risk-bearing economies.

2   **The diseconomies of large-scale production.**

3   **Reasons why small firms still exist** . . . The economies of small-scale production.

4   **Integration** . . . Horizontal and vertical integration, lateral integration, conglomerates and multi-national firms.

5   **Monopoly and competition** . . . Advantages and disadvantages of both monopoly and competitive firms.

1 THE ECONOMIES OF LARGE-SCALE PRODUCTION

(a) THE INCREASING SIZE OF FIRMS

Production is carried on by many firms, varying in size from sole trader to huge joint stock companies with thousands of shareholders. The trend has been for firms to become bigger and bigger. Some firms are taken over by others, others amalgamate. It is not unusual for entire industries to be dominated by a few large firms which may monopolize a particular sector of production, e.g.:

> *Banking:* Barclays, Lloyds, Midland, National Westminster, The Royal Bank of Scotland.
> *Vehicle production:* Ford, Austin-Rover (formerly British Leyland), General Motors (Vauxhall), Peugeot/Talbot.

Some firms may form a *cartel*, in which a group of firms get together with the aim of fixing prices and output in a particular industry. They aim to act as a *monopolist*, dominating the market and thus having the power to increase prices and reduce output against the interest of consumers. A monopolistic situation is often seen as undesirable, and the government has set up the *Monopolies and Mergers Commission* to investigate possible mergers which could lead to a monopoly. If there is such a likelihood, the government may prohibit these mergers.

Both in private enterprise and public enterprise, the main reason for the trend towards increasing size has been the economies of large-scale production. You should be fully aware of these economies. There are two types of economy of scale – internal and external. External economies of scale are dealt with on pp.63–5.

(b) THE INTERNAL ECONOMIES OF LARGE-SCALE PRODUCTION

Internal economies of scale are the advantages which come to a firm as a result of its decision to increase its size. All these will reduce the costs of production for the larger firm and make its products cheaper to consumers. There are several types of internal economies of scale for you to consider. They are:

(i) TECHNICAL ECONOMIES

–   Greater division of labour. See pp.57–8.
–   Large and expensive machinery can be purchased. Some machinery is indivisible, which means that it can be used economically only with large outputs.
–   Large machines can sometimes cut the costs per unit of output. They cater for a much larger output at only a slight increase in costs. This is called the economy of increased dimensions.
–   Large firms can afford to link processes so that production goes on as efficiently and economically as possible.
–   Large firms can afford to have the right size machinery at all stages of production, so that there are no hold-ups.

(ii) FINANCIAL ECONOMIES

–   It is easier to obtain large bank loans at lower interest rates.
–   The issue of shares and debentures. If the firm is a PLC (see p.93), it can issue shares and debentures on the Stock Exchange.

(iii) COMMERCIAL (OR MARKETING) ECONOMIES

–   The purchase of goods and materials in bulk (large quantities) at lower prices. The firm may receive discounts.
–   Selling large quantities is not that much more expensive in terms of administration.
–   Advertising on television or in the national newspapers at home or overseas.
–   Good packaging and free gifts and competitions to help sell the goods, although small firms also introduce such marketing practices.

(iv) MANAGERIAL ECONOMIES

–   The large firm can employ skilled managers.

–   Managers can specialize in certain activities, e.g. personnel manager, marketing manager and production manager.

(v) RESEARCH ECONOMIES

It is possible to afford research laboratories, employ scientists and make grants to universities to develop new and better techniques.

(vi) WELFARE ECONOMIES

Large firms can afford good working conditions, canteens and social and leisure facilities for the employees (small firms may also introduce such welfare facilities).

(vii) RISK-BEARING ECONOMIES

Large firms can reduce risks by producing different products and having several different supplies.

Despite all these advantages of size, there are disadvantages in being large; these are known as the diseconomies of large-scale production.

2 THE DISECONOMIES OF LARGE-SCALE PRODUCTION

(i)   Personal contact with staff and customers is lost.

(ii)   Workers and managers may not work so hard, regarding themselves as being less important in a large firm.

(iii) There are the disadvantages of division of labour.

(iv)   Decision-making is more difficult because of the larger management structure of the firm.

(v)   There is too much red tape and bureaucracy within the firm.

The largest UK enterprises	Turnover £ billion	Employees at home and abroad '000
British Petroleum	38.0	132
Shell Transport and Trading	24.4	n/a
BAT Industries	11.7	187
*Electricity Council	9.1	141
Imperial Chemical Industries	8.3	118
British National Oil Corporation	7.9	n/a
Shell UK	7.8	18
Esso UK	7.6	7
British Telecom	6.4	249
British Gas	5.9	103
Unilever plc	5.4	127

*Public corporation or nationalized industry
Source: *Britain An Economic Profile 1985* (Lloyds Bank)

Although the trend has been for firms to get larger in recent years, small firms still exist and indeed are more numerous than large firms. This is an important point for you to remember. The following reasons for the continuing existence of small firms should be considered.

3 REASONS WHY SMALL FIRMS STILL EXIST

The economies of small-scale production . . . The advantages of being small can be found on pp.89–90 under the 'advantages of the sole proprietor'.

Other reasons . . . In addition to the advantages of small-scale production:
(i)   they may not be able to raise the capital to expand;
(ii)   demand for the product they produce may be small;
(iii)   they cannot attract the good managers away from large firms;
(iv)   sometimes there is a need to adapt quickly to changes in demand; small firms tend to be found in those industries where quick decisions may have to be made (e.g. in agriculture, because of changes in the weather) or where a variety of goods produced is required (e.g. fashion) or where a personal service is needed (e.g. small retail shops).

MC1   In which of the following would large-scale production *not* be suitable?
(*a*)   where a personal service is required
(*b*)   where mass-production techniques are in use
(*c*)   where large amounts of capital investment is required
(*d*)   where there is a large demand
(*e*)   where standardized production techniques are established

MC2   Which of the following aspects of large-scale production is an advantage to the consumer?
(*a*)   greater profitability
(*b*)   standardized production
(*c*)   diseconomies of scale
(*d*)   lower prices
(*e*)   less competition

MC3   An organization of firms established for the purpose of controlling prices and output is a
(*a*)   monopoly
(*b*)   oligopoly
(*c*)   joint stock company
(*d*)   holding company
(*e*)   cartel

MC4 If a firm experiences economies of scale, then its
(a)   sales must be increasing
(b)   sales must be falling
(c)   profits must be increasing
(d)   average costs of production must be falling
(e)   average costs of production must be rising

MC5 Organizations that employ mass-production techniques need
(a)   to employ more skilled labour
(b)   to have branches in many different countries
(c)   to produce a wide variety of products
(d)   to sell their products throughout the world
(e)   a large market for their products

4 INTEGRATION

Firms may become bigger by amalgamation or integration. There are two main forms of integration: horizontal and vertical integration.

(a) HORIZONTAL INTEGRATION

Firms may become bigger by amalgamating with other firms which are the same stage of the same production process. For instance, the National Provincial Bank and the Westminster Bank amalgamated to become the National Westminster Bank.

(b) VERTICAL INTEGRATION

Firms may become bigger by amalgamating with other firms which are at different stages of the same production process. For instance, a brewery may own the hopfield and the public houses. A chocolate manufacturer may own a cocoa plantation. There are two types of vertical integration:

(i) Backward integration This occurs when a firm amalgamates with the suppliers of its material or component parts.

(ii) Forward integration This occurs when a firm amalgamates with those which sell and market its products.

(c) ADVANTAGES OF INTEGRATION

(i)   Achieves economies of scale.
(ii)   May achieve a large share of the market. Current opinion suggest that this is often undesirable because of the dangers of forming a monopoly.
(iii)   Vertical integration backwards will ensure that the firm gets

its materials at the right time, in the right place, at the right quality and in the right quantity.

(iv)   Vertical integration forwards will likewise ensure that the firms can sell its goods at the right time, etc.

(v)   Integration is likely to prevent suppliers making a large profit.

(vi)   The firms become large so that they can compete with large multinational firms. These are large firms based in many countries of the world, e.g. Ford, IBM, Shell.

(d) DISADVANTAGES OF INTEGRATION

(i)   Large firms suffer from the diseconomies of large-scale production.

(ii)   They may form monopolies which may not be in the consumers' interests.

(iii)   In recent years the performance of large firms has not always been impressive. A feeling may be growing that 'big is bad' and 'small is beautiful'.

(e) LATERAL INTEGRATION

This is a merger between firms where they have common sources of raw materials or market outlets or have similar products, e.g. Cadbury-Schweppes.

(f) CONGLOMERATES (DIVERSIFICATION)

A conglomerate is one in which a firm integrates with others, and very often there is no conceivable direct link. The Imperial Tobacco Company, for example, owns Ross Frozen Foods, whilst the British Match Corporation owns Wilkinson Sword. Lloyds Bank owns a finance house, an estate agent and has interests in subsidiary firms both in this country and abroad.

Apart from the advantage of achieving the economies of scale, the conglomerate can diversify its product range and not rely on one specific type of good. This would apply particularly where a firm has already absorbed a large proportion of the available market.

(g) MULTINATIONAL FIRMS

These are organizations which are based in many different countries. It is likely that the parent company is based on one country and has subsidiaries in numerous other countries, e.g. Ford, Beechams, General Motors, Unilever, etc. Multinationals achieve the economies of large-scale production, having more than one market to satisfy, often with a wide range of products suiting 'local' needs. They are frequently criticized for damaging the 'home firms' and it is possible that they may accumulate undesirable political strength in that country. Thus the wealth and power of the multinational may be used in its own selfish interest, with the attendant risk of meddling in a country's politics.

MC6   A tyre company taking control over a rubber plantation would be an example of
(*a*)   economies of scale
(*b*)   a cartel
(*c*)   vertical integration
(*d*)   horizontal integration
(*e*)   diversification

MC7   Which of the following is an example of horizontal integration?
(*a*)   a tyre company merges with a rubber plantation
(*b*)   a car firm takes over a chain of garages
(*c*)   one bank merges with another
(*d*)   a tobacco company takes over a brewery
(*e*)   a washing machine manufacturer amalgamates with a freezer manufacturer

MC8   A multinational organization is one which is/has
(*a*)   shareholders in more than one country
(*b*)   branches in more than one country
(*c*)   nationalized
(*d*)   based in Britain but employs many nationalities
(*e*)   based in the European Community

5 MONOPOLY AND COMPETITION

In some industries there are many firms, some large and others small, which are competing against each other. This is termed competition. In other industries there may be a single firm (termed a monopoly) or a few very large firms (termed oligopoly).

(a) MONOPOLY

Although monopoly has been defined as one single firm being the industry, in practice a legal definition is one firm controlling at least 25 per cent of the industry's output. Monopolist industries are characterized by a lack of close substitutes for the commodity and presenting barriers to the entry of new firms. Such barriers to entry might include possession of a patent, restrictive agreements with supply or market outlets and price-cutting to drive away competition. There are four main foundations of monopoly power:
–   national monopolies . . . when the firm has sole supply of a

raw material or commodity, owing to natural deposits or climatic reasons.

–   statutory monopolies . . . when the monopoly is supported by an Act of Parliament, as in the case of the nationalized industries.

–   technological monopolies . . . when the firm is so big that it alone enjoys the economies of scale.

–   local monopolies . . . a monopoly may exist in the locality, as in the case of the village shop.

(i) ADVANTAGES OF MONOPOLY

–   Monopolies tend to be large and enjoy the economies of scale. Average costs and prices to the consumer fall.

–   Monopolies cut out the wastes of duplicated goods and services.

–   Monopolies can afford to spend money on research and improvements.

(ii) DISADVANTAGES OF MONOPOLY

–   Owing to lack of competition, the monopolist raises prices and the quality of the commodity falls.

–   Monopolies may be too large and suffer from the diseconomies of scale. Average costs and prices to the consumer rise.

–   Monopolies may adopt unfair practices to keep out new firms. These are called barriers to entry.

(b) COMPETITION

Competition is based on the principles of perfect competition. This is a theoretical situation where there are many small firms, there is freedom of exit and entry into the industry and no government interference with firms. Competition approximates to this theoretical situation.

(i) ADVANTAGES OF COMPETITION

–   There is a wide variety and choice of commodities available to consumers.

–   Firms have to be aware of their competitors, so the quality and price of the commodity has to be attended to carefully.

–   Firms tend to be small and enjoy the economies of small-scale production.

(ii) DISADVANTAGES OF COMPETITION

–   There may be a waste of duplicated goods and services.

–   Small firms may not be able to afford the money for research and improvements.

– Small firms cannot enjoy the economies of large-scale production, which may mean that costs and prices to consumers will be high.

It may seem to you that there are a great many contradictory advantages and disadvantages regarding competition and monopoly. You may feel that it is impossible to state which is the best situation – monopoly or competition. Of course, some monopolies may have many desirable traits. However, other monopolies may be mainly bad. Indeed, the government tends to believe that most monopolies are on balance bad. Consequently, much anti-monopoly legislation has been passed and a Monopolies and Mergers Commission has been set up to control the activities of monopolies.

MC9 Which of the following industries is a monopoly supplier in the UK?
(a) car manufacturing
(b) television broadcasting
(c) brewing
(d) oil refining
(e) railways

MC10 A market situation where there are only a few large firms in existence is known as
(a) oligopoly
(b) competition
(c) monopoly
(d) integration
(e) cartel

EXTENDED WRITING QUESTIONS

1 (a) Explain the meaning of the terms
(i) 'economies of scale'
(ii) 'diseconomies of scale'
(b) Why do small firms continue to survive?
(c) (i) How and (ii) why do firms increase their size?

2 (a) Give the main features of a multinational corporation.
(b) Why have businesses been developed in this form?
(c) How may their existence create problems for national governments?

3 (a) What is meant by
(i) internal economies of scale?
and (ii) external economies of scale?
(b) Outline the (i) internal economies of scale and (ii) external economies which might apply to a large motor vehicle manufacturer.
(c) 'In some industries the optimum size of firm is small.' Explain this statement.

4 (a)   Distinguish between the various forms of integration.

(b)   Why do companies integrate?

(c)   For what reasons may the government encourage the development of small firms?

Answer

(a)   You need to distinguish mainly between horizontal and vertical integration. Horizontal integration is the merging of two firms at the same stage in the same production process, e.g. two car manufacturers. Vertical integration is the merging of two firms at different stages in the same production process, e.g. a motor vehicle manufacturer and a brake components firm. Mention backward and forward integration. Also mention conglomerates, diversification and lateral integration.

(b)   There are different reasons for horizontal and vertical integration and diversification. Refer to pp.79–81. Main reasons include to achieve economies of scale and to achieve monopoly power.

(c)   As a source of new ideas, to create jobs, for contribution to national output and balance of payment, a small firm today may develop into a large firm tomorrow, more flexibility and variety. More competition (see advantages of competition).

5 (a)   Distinguish (i) monopoly and competition (ii) private monopoly and public monopoly.

(b)   'Monopoly is always against the public interest.' Discuss this statement.

(c)   How has the government attempted to inhibit the growth of private monopolies?

DATA RESPONSE

Scottish and Newcastle, one of the six largest brewing companies in the country, proposed to take over Matthew Brown, a substantial regional brewer based in Lancashire, selling mainly in the North-West. In deciding whether the merger would be against the public interest, the [Monopolies and Mergers] Commission looked at the likely effects on competition, on prices and whether they might be increased in the combined company's pubs after the merger, on consumer choice and service to the public, and on employment. (J. P. L. Scott (Monopolies and Mergers Commission))

(a)   The proposed merger between Scottish and Newcastle and Matthew Brown is an example of which type of integration?

(b)   Describe the role of the Monopolies and Mergers Commission.

(*c*) What advantages may be expected if the proposed merger is successful
> (i) for consumers?
> (ii) for producers?

(*d*) What disadvantages may be expected if the proposed merger is successful
> (i) for consumers?
> (ii) for producers?

Answers to multiple-choice questions:

MC1	(*a*)	**MC6**	(*c*)
MC2	(*d*)	**MC7**	(*c*)
MC3	(*e*)	**MC8**	(*b*)
MC4	(*d*)	**MC9**	(*e*)
MC5	(*e*)	**MC10**	(*a*)

THE STRUCTURE
OF INDUSTRY:
THE PRIVATE SECTOR

CONTENTS

In this chapter we examine the meaning of private enterprise (public enterprise is dealt with in Chapter 6). The chapter is divided into a study of each individual type of firm to be found in private enterprise:

1   **Sole traders** (or proprietors).

2   **Partnerships** Two types: ordinary partnerships and limited partnerships.,

3   **The co-operative movement** Consumer co-operatives and producer co-operatives.

4   **Joint stock (or limited) companies** Distinguishing features; two types of joint stock companies: private joint stock companies and public joint stock companies (plcs), advantages and disadvantages. How joint stock companies are formed, raising finance, ownership and control.

5   **Holding companies.**

The UK economy is a mixed economy in that it is made up of two types of industries, those which are owned by private investors and those whch are owned by the state. You must be aware of this fundamental and important distinction and be prepared for questions which require comparisons of the different aspects of private and public enterprise – often called the private and public sectors.

All firms in the private sector have one objective: to make profits.

1   SOLE TRADERS (OR PROPRIETORS)

The sole trader is a one-man business, for example some retail shops (newsagents, greengrocers, etc.) and window-cleaners. Sole traders are found particularly in the areas of business where a personal service is desirable, or quick decisions need to be made.

(i)   ADVANTAGES

-    They keep all the profit for themselves.
-    They are their own boss and have independence.
-    They can make quick decisions.

–   They provide a personal service for customers and staff.
–   They enjoy the economies of small-scale production (see pp.78).

(ii) DISADVANTAGES

–   They are often not able to take holidays and there may be problems if they are ill.
–   There is no limited liability (see p.93).
–   They cannot enjoy the advantages of economies of large-scale production (see p.76–7).

(iii) THE RAISING OF CAPITAL

Money is needed to buy equipment for the running of the business. The sole trader could raise this from his own savings, with loans from relatives or friends, by 'ploughing back' profits into the firm, or by small bank loans.

2 PARTNERSHIPS

If a sole trader wishes to expand the firm, he or she may form a partnership. There are two types – an ordinary (or general) partnership and limited partnership.

(a) THE ORDINARY PARTNERSHIP

An ordinary partnership usually consists of between two and twenty partners. However, where large amounts of capital investment or expertise are required – e.g. an accountants' practice – more than twenty partners are permitted.

(i) ADVANTAGES

–   Partnerships can usually raise more capital than sole traders.
–   The different partners can contribute different skills and experience.
–   Business affairs still remain private.

(ii) DISADVANTAGES

–   They do not have limited liability (see p.83).
–   They still tend to be quite small and cannot enjoy the economies of large-scale production.
–   All the partners have to be consulted when decision are made.
–   Profits have to be shared (usually equally unless otherwise stated).

–   Decisions are binding on all partners.

(b) THE LIMITED PARTNERSHIP

This consists of between two and twenty partners with limited liability. However, at least one partner in a limited partnership must be a general or ordinary partner. This means that he or she will not have limited liability and will therefore carry the full burden of paying off debts, even out of personal belongings if the partnership fails. Limited partnerships are not popular nowadays. Most firms, if they wish to raise capital, will form a private company.

(i) ADVANTAGES

–   Because the limited partner has limited liability, that partner is taking less of a risk and may therefore contribute more capital.
–   He or she still takes a share in the profits.

(ii) DISADVANTAGES

–   Only the general partners have a say in the running of the partnership and making decisions. ('Sleeping' partners take no part in decision-making but still enjoy a share of the profits.)
–   The limited partners' share of the profits will probably be less, because they are taking less of a risk.
–   The limited partners are unable to withdraw even part of their capital unless the general ordinary partners agree.
–   Partnerships are most evident in the professions – e.g. doctors, dentists, barristers and solicitors – because the rules of the professional bodies (British Medical Association, the Law Society, etc.) prohibit their members from forming themselves into private limited companies.

3 THE CO-OPERATIVE MOVEMENT

In Britain there are two broad types of co-operative society:

(a) CONSUMER CO-OPERATIVES

(i) THE CO-OPERATIVE RETAIL SOCIETIES

These date back to the 'Rochdale Pioneers' of 1844, when a group of people in that Lancashire town co-operated together to buy goods in bulk. These were then sold to consumers in the area at prices below those charged elsewhere. This important principle can still be seen today in the co-operative movement, there being about 120 separate societies in the country with some 10 million members.

(ii) RAISING OF CAPITAL

An important aspect of the movement is its open membership. The share lists never close and shares (usually of £1 denominations) may be purchased by anyone. There is, however, a maximum share owner-ship. Whatever his or her holding, a shareholder is entitled to only one vote per resolution at meetings. Further important points include:

–   Shares may be redeemed at their face value – their purchase price – as and when required.

–   The liability of all members is limited.

–   The shares are not sold on the Stock Exchange, share certifi-cates are not issued, and shares can be purchased only at the local societies.

(iii) DISPOSAL OF PROFITS

A proportion of available profits is ploughed back into the business, the remainder being distributed amongst the members in proportion to their purchases. This is usually by way of 'dividend stamps' which may be later redeemed for cash, though these are being phased out for lower prices. Shareholders also receive a dividend on the shares they own.

(iv) OWNERSHIP

Each of the retail societies has a separate existence, although some have merged to form a larger unit known as the Co-operative Retail Services Ltd in order to reap the benefits of large-scale enterprise. Nevertheless, each society is owned by its members, who are able to appoint its own Committee of Management.

(v) THE CO-OPERATIVE WHOLESALE SOCIETY (CWS)

This was formed in 1863 to supply retail societies with products for resale. Today the retail societies purchase about two-thirds of their supplies from this source, the remainder from the private and public sectors. Other activities of the CWS include:

–   manufacturing their own goods and food products;

–   farming both in this country and overseas;

–   travel agencies and hotels, printing, publishing, laundries, etc.;

–   controlling the operation of CWS-based banking and insur-ance offices;

–   assisting the retail societies by undertaking national adver-tising campaigns, research projects, etc.

Control of the CWS is in the hands of the retail societies themselves. They contribute most of the capital and elect the Board of Directors. Their voting power is proportional to the value of their purchases from the CWS.

Changes in the Co-operative movement over recent years include:
– less emphasis and concentration on food sales and a move to other areas of retailing;
– a growth through amalgamations of larger societies in order to compete on a more equal footing with the other large retail organizations, hypermarkets, etc.;
– more local and national advertising – particularly through the press and TV;
– the introduction of modern retailing to members and non-members.

(b) PRODUCER CO-OPERATIVES

These are less numerous than consumer co-operatives. In this form of co-operation it is the employees who provide the capital and take the risks. The company is owned by the workers, who provide the capital, and profits are shared. This type of co-operation is more widespread on the Continent.

Although firm such as sole traders and partnerships are numerous within the economy, another important type of firm is the joint stock company.

4 JOINT STOCK (OR LIMITED) COMPANIES

(a) DISTINGUISHING FEATURES

The distinguishing feature of joint stock companies is that they issue shares and have limited liability. This means that in the event of a company going out of business, shareholders will lose only the money they have invested in the company, and not their personal assets. (Compare this with a sole trader or partnership.)

LIMITED LIABILITY

This is a great advantage to joint stock companies. It enables them to raise more capital, since investors are more willing to buy shares in the knowledge that at the worst they lose only their investment and not personal possessions as well.

(b) TYPES OF JOINT STOCK COMPANY

There are two types: a private joint stock company and a public joint stock company.

Examiners often refer to these as limited companies, or private companies, or public companies. The latter may also be termed PLCs. (The operations of companies have been affected by the 1981 Companies Act.)

(i) The private joint stock company has five distinguishing features:

–   at least two shareholders, with no maximum;
–   shares are not offered to the public on the Stock Exchange;
–   the transfer of shares can take place only with the agreement of all the shareholders;
–   it is smaller but more numerous than public companies – it is often a family-run business.
–   it is free from many of the legal requirements of the public company.

(ii) A public company has the following distinguishing features:
–   it must have a minimum of two shareholders – there is no limit to the maximum number;
–   it issues shares to the public on the Stock Exchange;
–   it tends to be larger and not so numerous as private companies;
–   the public company's affairs are public;
–   the words Public Limited Company or plc after the company's name;
–   the minimum share issue is £50,000.

(c) ADVANTAGES AND DISADVANTAGES

(i) ADVANTAGES

–   Large amounts of capital can be raised.
–   Each shareholder has limited liability.
–   Shares are easily transferable.
–   There are legal requirements to be satisfied, safeguarding the shareholder.
–   Accounts are made public.
–   It may enjoy economies of scale.

(ii) DISADVANTAGES

–   It suffers the diseconomies and disadvantages of large-scale production.
–   There may be a divorce between ownership and control (see p.99).

(d) HOW JOINT STOCK COMPANIES ARE FORMED

The company must prepare the following documents in the interest of shareholders:

(i) THE MEMORANDUM OF ASSOCIATION

This must be sent to the Registrar of Companies. It would include:
–   the name of the company, with 'limited' (or plc if public) as the last word;

- the location of the registered office;
- the objects of the company;
- a statement that liability is limited;
- amounts of shares and types of shares to be issued.

This Memorandum must be signed by at least two people and they must agree to take shares in the comnpany.

(ii) THE ARTICLES OF ASSOCIATION

This would explain how the internal running of the company would be controlled, and would include:
- the powers of the managing director;
- how meetings are to be organized;
- how shares are to be issued and transferred;
- how profit will be divided.

The Memorandum and Articles of Association, together with a statement of authorized capital (i.e. the amount of shares it might issue) are sent to the Registrar of Companies. If all is in order the Registrar will issue a Certificate of Incorporation.

(iii) THE CERTIFICATE OF INCORPORATION

Issued by the Registrar of Companies, this recognizes the company and gives it permission to begin trading. It must be displayed in the company's registered office.

(iv) THE PROSPECTUS

This applies only to public companies when they are about to set up in business. It invites the public to take shares in the company. A copy is filed with the Registrar. It contains the names and addresses of directors with all details likely to be of interest to investors so that they can assess the prospects of the company.

MC1 The word 'limited' at the end of a firm's name means
(*a*)   it can carry out only certain activities
(*b*)   shareholders are not liable for paying all the debts of the company
(*c*)   the capital is limited
(*d*)   shareholders cannot lose the money they have paid for their shares
(*e*)   there can be only fifty shareholders

MC2 The capital of a limited company is provided by
(*a*)   the partners
(*b*)   the debtors

(c)   the creditors
(d)   the directors
(e)   the shareholders

MC3   An important advantage of the limited company is
(a)   it cannot be sued in law
(b)   it is not bound by any Act of Parliament
(c)   it can have any number of shareholders between two and twenty
(d)   it continues to exist even though its shares change hands
(e)   it is owned by the government

MC4   When the public are invited to subscribe to a new share issue, the information concerning the issue is given in the
(a)   Memorandum
(b)   Articles
(c)   Prospectus
(d)   Debenture
(e)   Certificate of Incorporation

(e) RAISING CAPITAL

In this section we examine the four main ways by which joint stock companies raise capital: issue shares, issue debentures, plough-back of profits, and bank loans.

(i) SHARES

There are various types of share which can be issued, but the company must follow the Memorandum of Association. A shareholder may receive a share in the profits depending upon company policy, this reward being called a dividend.

The types of share are: ordinary shares, preference shares, cumulative preference shares, participating preference shares and deferred or founders' shares. A company may issue different types of share to attract different types of shareholder and raise more capital. Some investors are cautious and have only a small amount to invest. These people are likely to purchase cumulative preference shares, where the risks are less. Others investors are willing to take a risk in their pursuit of big dividends. These people would probably purchase ordinary shares. As well as individuals purchasing shares, the institutions are important purchasers of shares; these include banks, insurance companies, investment trusts, pension funds and, indeed, other companies. These are called institutional investors.

Ordinary shares (or equities)
Advantages In years of very good profits they may achieve large dividends because they do not have fixed interest rates limiting their dividend payment.

Owners of ordinary shares are often the only type of shareholder who can vote at the annual general meeting (AGM) of the board of directors and shareholders.

Disadvantages They are last in the queue of shareholders when dividends are being paid out.

In bad years, when only small profits are made, the ordinary shareholder may not receive any divident at all – for this reason ordinary shares are often called risk capital.

Preference shares
Advantages The preference shareholder has a claim on profits before the ordinary shareholder.

They are fixed-interest dividend shares, which means a guaranteed dividend.

Disadvantages They carry fixed-interest dividends – this could be a disadvantage when very good profits are made and the dividend going to the preference shareholders is small in relation to that being paid on ordinary shares.

Preference shareholders often cannot vote at the AGM and therefore have no say in the running of the company.

Cumulative preference shares (cumulative means increasingly adding together)
Advantages As for preference shares. Nowadays all preference shares are cumulative unless otherwise stated; when they do not receive the correct amount of dividend in any one year or years of poor profits, they would catch up on these missed dividends eventually in a year of good profits.

Disadvantages As for preference shares.

Participating preference shares
Their advantages and disadvantages are the same as for preference shares. However, they have the additional advantages of their entitlement to a bonus from profits in good profit years, after the ordinary shareholders have received sufficient dividend.

Deferred or founders' shares
These are usually taken up by the founders of the company. They would receive a dividend after all the claims of all the other shareholders have been met. In practice their shares are transferred to one of the other types of share described above after the company has become established.

Why buy shares?
In order to earn a dividend.

To gain control of the company by buying the shares entitling the holder to a vote.

To speculate – hope that the market price of the share will rise so that it may be sold later at a profit.

(ii) DEBENTURES

These are loans to the company, mainly from banks and other financial institutions as well as private investors. They carry a fixed rate of interest and this must be paid out whether the company makes a profit or a loss. They carry a low risk and are bought by investors who are cautious and looking for not only low, but safe, returns. Like shares, they can be purchased on the Stock Exchange.

(iii) PLOUGH-BACK OF PROFITS

When profits are made the company might pay all these in dividends to shareholders. It could and usually does – retain some to finance spending on machinery, to provide for further production, employment, etc. This is the most usual way of financing expansion.

(iv) BORROWING FROM THE BANK

Joint stock companies may be able to raise money by borrowing on a loan account from a bank. They may also be able to borrow on a short-term basis from the bank by going into overdraft on their current account. For more details on the loan account, overdraft and current account, see Chapter 11 on banking.

MC5 The ordinary shares of a company are known as
(*a*)   working capital
(*b*)   equity capital
(*c*)   reserve capital
(*d*)   fixed capital
(*e*)   circulating capital

MC6 A share which carries a fixed rate of dividend is known as
(*a*)   a debenture
(*b*)   a preference share
(*c*)   an ordinary share
(*d*)   a founder's share
(*e*)   a gilt-edged security

MC7 Shareholders receive a share of the profits of a company in the form of
(*a*)   interest
(*b*)   dividends
(*c*)   premiums
(*d*)   rent
(*e*)   salaries

The final aspect of joint stock companies you need to be aware of concerns who owns and who controls them.

(f) OWNERSHIP AND CONTROL OF A JOINT STOCK COMPANY

The owners of the company are its shareholders. These elect a board of directors, headed by a chairman. The board may meet regularly and make broad decisions applying to the running of the company. The directors and chairman are often some of the largest shareholders. However, the day-to-day running of the joint stock company may be in the hand of a managing director. He need not be a shareholder and is appointed by the board.

It could therefore be that the owners of the company may not have day-to-day control of its affairs. Indeed, the mass of shareholders may meet only once a year – many not even bothering to turn up – at the AGM. This often leads to a divorce between ownership and control.

Joint stock companies are an extremely important part of the syllabus, and you can expect questions to be set on this topic. It is already been noted that you may be asked to make a comparison between public companies and public corporations. You may also be asked to compare joint stock companies with other private enterprise firms.

MC8 The members of the board of a public company are chosen by
(a)   a government minister
(b)   the managing director
(c)   the founders of the company
(d)   the Registrar of Companies
(e)   the shareholders

5 HOLDING COMPANIES

An important aspect of ownership and control of joint stock companies which you need to be able to discuss is the holding company. These are companies which gain control of other companies and frequently form conglomerates (see page 80). They can do this by gaining over half the ordinary shares in the other company (known subsequently as a subsidiary). Indeed, if only a small percentage of ordinary shareholders turn up at the AGM it could be possible to pass resolutions not in the interest of the shareholders in that company, particularly if a few hold a large number of shares.

(i) REASONS FOR FORMING HOLDING COMPANIES

There may be three advantages in forming a holding company:

–   It would allow the firms to achieve the economies of large-scale production.

–   It could prevent competition and form a monopoly. A monopoly is a firm that dominates an industry and can set prices without fear of competition. This may be an advantage for the company but may result in high prices for consumers.

–   The firm could, through a process known as rationalization, close down the loss-making sectors and concentrate on those sectors which produce the highest return.

(ii) CRITICISMS OF HOLDING COMPANIES

The most important points made against holding companies are:

–   They could form monopolies.

–   They gain control of a whole group of companies for a relatively small amount of money, e.g.

COMPANY A: Capital includes £1 million worth of ordinary shares and debentures worth £1 million. Controls

COMPANY B: Capital includes £500,000 worth of ordinary shares and debentures worth £250,000.

Another company may be able to gain control of Company A by purchasing over half its ordinary shares for over £500,000. For this amount it would have control of Company B as well.

–   A company may be bought by purchasing over half its ordinary shares. Then its assets (premises, furniture, machinery) may be sold off – this is called asset-stripping. This would create unemployment. Holding companies are required to make clear to the public their control of subsidiaries. Examples of holding companies: Sears (Holdings) plc, Unilever plc, Imperial Chemical Industries Ltd, etc.

MC9   Which of the following will definitely not be an aim of a holding company gaining control of a subsidiary?
(*a*)   to encourage more competition
(*b*)   to achieve a monopoly
(*c*)   to enjoy the economies of scale
(*d*)   to rationalize the industry
(*e*)   to sell off the assets

MC10   Which of the following is not a part of the private enterprise sector?
(*a*)   sole proprietors
(*b*)   limited partnerships
(*c*)   public corporations
(*d*)   public companies
(*e*)   private companies

EXTENDED WRITING QUESTIONS

1 (*a*) Explain the significance of plc (public limited company) after the name of a business.
   (*b*) Discuss the importance of this term to
        (i) the company's shareholders and
        (ii) the expansion of the business
   (*c*) How does a plc differ from a private limited company?

   Answer
   (*a*) The term plc shows that the firm is a public joint stock company with limited liability. You should now explain the meaning of limited liability. The firm is a public company (not a public corporation). Discuss the main features, including the number of shareholders, ownership, control, raising of capital, disposal of profits.
   (*b*)   (i) Discuss the significance of limited liability to shareholders – the advantages. The ability to buy and sell shares at known (quoted) prices on the Stock Exchange. Liability of shareholders is limited to the amount of money they have used to purchase shares.
            (ii) The company will find it easier to raise capital in order to expand. Investors will be more willing to risk their capital.
   (*c*) To answer this you need to discuss the distinguishing features of a plc compared with a private company. For instance, shares in a plc are bought and sold on the stock Exchange, plcs tend to be larger (minimum share issure of £50,000) and more numerous, shareholders have to be invited to purchase shares in a private company, the financial affairs of a private company are much more private.

2 (*a*) What are the special features of a co-operative retail society?
   (*b*) Why has the number of retailing societies declined very rapidly?
   (*c*) How have the retail co-operative societies benefited from this reduction in numbers?

3 (*a*) What is a holding company?
   (*b*) Name and describe the different types of share issued by public companies.
   (*c*) Explain the advantages of each type of share to
        (i) the shareholders and
        (ii) the company.

4 Consider a business owned by a single proprietor and a business owned by a public company.
   (*a*) How might each business raise the necessary capital?
   (*b*) How is each business managed?
   (*c*) What happens in each case when profits are made?
   (*d*) The single proprietor may decide to form a private limited company to run his business. Give reasons why he might do so.

5 (*a*) Examine the main features of
        (i) sole proprietor

(ii) partnership.
(b)   What are the main ways in which firms in private enterprise may raise capital?
(c)   State the main differences between
(i) public and private enterprise, and
(ii) public companies and public corporations.

DATA RESPONSE   Study the passage below and then answer questions (a) to (e).

Havant plc is one of two toy manufacturers in Portsmouth. The company have capital from investors of £450,000 divided into:
£300,000 ordinary shares c 50p each.
£100,000 cumulative preference shares of £1 each, attracting 7% return.
£50,000 of loan capital in 6% debentures of £1 each.
After all other payments have been made, the company has the following amounts available for distribution to shareholders over a three-year period:
Year 1   £9,000
Year 2   £15,500
Year 3   £43,000
The company, encouraged by its good performance in Year 3, is considering expanding. There are two possibilities:
1   Take over Emsworth plc, the other local toy manufacturer.
2   Establish a new toy manufacturing company in a development area over 100 miles away in South Wales.

(a)   What is the type of integration being considered by the company?
(b)   What is the main advantage for shareholders of Havant plc of having limited liability?
(c)   If Havant plc decides to take over Emsworth plc, give two advantages which may be expected.
(d)   What factors should be considered by the directors of Havant plc when deciding whether to build a new factory in South Wales (a development area)?
(e)   Calculate how much the debenture holders, cumulative preference shareholders and ordinary shareholders receive in each year.

Answer to multiple-choice questions:

MC1	(b)		MC6	(b)
MC2	(e)		MC7	(b)
MC3	(d)		MC8	(e)
MC4	(c)		MC9	(a)
MC5	(b)		MC10	(c)

THE STRUCTURE OF INDUSTRY: THE PUBLIC SECTOR

CONTENTS

Contents

This chapter concentrates on the public sector or public enterprise. We cover the following areas:

1 **What is the public sector?** . . . The public sector is more than just nationalized industries.

2 **For and against nationalization** (public corporations).

3 **The raising of capital, disposal of profits, and ownership and control.**

4 **Local authorities** . . . Functions, control, financing (rates), alternatives to rates.

5 **Privatization.**

1 WHAT IS THE PUBLIC SECTOR?

The public sector is that part of the UK's mixed economy owned by the state and controlled by the government. It is different from the private sector, which includes firms and businesses owned by private individuals (or entrepreneurs) and is often called private enterprise. The UK is said to be a mixed economy because it consists of both public and private sectors. Students should be able to compare public enterprise with private enterprise.

The public sector includes:

(i)   The public services provided by government such as the navy, army, police, education, health and social security services which are run by government departments.

(ii)   Nationalized industries – also termed public corporations, e.g. British Rail. These should not be confused with the public companies or plcs (see p.93–4), Nationalized industries are government owned. The following are examples: power: Central Electricity Generating Board (CEGB); banking: Bank of England; industry: British Steel; transport: British Rail.

(iii)   Services provided by local authorities.

(iv)   Bodies and agencies set up by the government, e.g. the Monopolies and Mergers Commission.

(v)   The government also has large shareholdings in some public companies, e.g. British Petroleum.

MC1   A public enterprise is distinguished from a private enterprise by whether
(*a*)   it is making a profit
(*b*)   it has issued fixed-interest capital
(*c*)   it is owned by more or fewer than twenty persons
(*d*)   it is owned by the government
(*e*)   it makes a loss

MC2   The main difference between a public company and a public corporation is that:
(*a*)   the former is always small, the latter usually much larger
(*b*)   the former raises capital only through the Stock Exchange, the latter only through the taxpayer
(*c*)   the former is controlled by the government, the latter by the shareholders
(*d*)   the former is privately owned whilst the latter is publicly owned
(*e*)   there is no difference, since both organizations are the same

When an industry is nationalized, this does not mean that the holdings of existing shareholders are confiscated. These shareholders are given compensation by the exchange of their shares for government stocks in the newly formed nationalized industry. The main period of nationalization was between 1945 and 1951 when the then Labour government took over the control of coal mines, railways, some British airlines, electricity, gas, steel, and some transport. Nationalization still takes place from time to time, depending upon the type of government in power. There has in recent years been a move towards de-nationalization or privatization – e.g. British Telecom – and this is dealt with in more detail on pp.114-16.

You are probably aware that nationalization is a controversial topic and people may be strongly in favour of or against state involvement in industry, etc. The purpose of the following section is to outline the most commonly used arguments.

2   FOR AND AGAINST NATIONALIZATION (PUBLIC CORPORATIONS)

(a) ARGUMENTS IN FAVOUR OF NATIONALIZATION

(i) TO ACHIEVE ECONOMIES OF LARGE-SCALE PRODUCTION

Nationalized industries tend to be large and can enjoy the advantages of large size (see pp.75–7).

(ii) THE 'COMMANDING HEIGHTS OF THE ECONOMY' ARGUMENT

Certain industries are very important to the economy, e.g. power, steel, transport and coal. If the government wishes to gain and keep control over the economy, these industries may well need to be nationalized.

(iii) TO AVOID PRIVATE MONOPOLIES

One of the disadvantages of private enterprise is that it may lead to a private monopoly. Such a development has disadvantages to the consumer. Prices are said to be higher, output and investment may be of lower quality and there may be no variety or choice open to consumers.

(iv) WHERE MUCH CAPITAL IS NEEDED

Certain industries need to provide millions of pounds' worth of specialist buildings and machinery, e.g. a modern steelworks or power station. Private enterprise may not be able to afford such large undertakings for an industry of prime importance to the economy.

(v) CERTAIN INDUSTRIES ARE OPERATED BETTER WHEN ORGANIZED ON A NATIONAL BASIS

When railways began in the 1830s they were controlled by over a 100 small companies. This had disadvantages – passengers frequently had to change trains and there were many different rail gauges, etc. It is better to run railways on a national basis to avoid such inefficiencies. A similar argument applies to electricity, gas and other service industries such as the Post Office, water authorities, etc.

(vi) IT MAY BE UNWISE FROM THE POINT OF VIEW OF NATIONAL SECURITY FOR AN INDUSTRY TO BE IN THE HANDS OF PRIVATE ENTERPRISE

The provision of nuclear power should not be in the hands of private individuals or organizations, for obvious reasons.

(vii) SOCIAL

The government may wish to nationalize an industry which may have run into financial problems and is in danger of closing down. For instance, if well-known firms such as Austin-Rover and Rolls-Royce Aero-engines (privatized in 1987) were to have closed down this would have caused much undesirable unemployment (and loss of potential export earnings).

(viii) POLITICAL

When in power, Labour governments tend to be in favour of nationalization. This is usually part of their political programme, since they believe that the basic industries should be in government rather than private control.

(b) ARGUMENTS AGAINST NATIONALIZATION

(i) POLITICAL

Conservative governments tend to be against state intervention and nationalization. Since 1979 the government has been committed to a policy of privatization (or de-nationalization). Consequently some previously nationalized industries have been returned to the private sector, e.g. The National Freight Corporation (now the National Freight Consortium), Sealink (now British Ferries), Amersham International, British Telecom, British Gas, Rolls-Royce Aero-engines, etc. Mrs Thatcher's Conservative government believes in the advantages of competition and private enterprise and is opposed to nationalization and public enterprise.

(ii) NATIONALIZED INDUSTRIES SUFFER FROM THE DISECONOMIES OF LARGE-SCALE PRODUCTION

By their very nature they tend to be big and may therefore suffer from the disadvantages of being too large. See pp.77–8 on diseconomies of scale.

(iii) THERE IS A LACK OF PROFIT MOTIVE WHICH RESULTS IN INEFFICIENCY AND LOSS-MAKING

Nationalized industries fail to meet targets set and become too large, overstaffed and bureaucratic. They do not enjoy the advantages of competition.

(iv) THERE IS TOO MUCH POLITICAL INTERFERENCE

The government interferes in pricing and investment policies, often to achieve social objectives.

(v) NATIONALIZED INDUSTRIES FORM STATE OR PUBLIC MONOPOLIES

They may suffer from the same disadvantages as private monopolies, and because of their size these are more pronounced. Nationalized industries may charge a high price for a poor product.

(vi) PUBLIC ACCOUNTABILITY

Nationalized industries are always in the public eye and their results are investigated by both Parliament and the media. This may make managers overcautious; therefore decisions will never be exciting or imaginative because of the risks involved.

3 RAISING CAPITAL, DISPOSING OF PROFITS, OWNERSHIP AND CONTROL OF NATIONALIZED INDUSTRIES

This section discusses how nationalized industries raise the capital to carry on business, and in the event of a profit being made it illustrates what in fact happens to that profit. Finally it examines who in fact owns the nationalized industries and how they are controlled.

Students should be aware that questions set requiring a comparison of public and private enterprise (or public corporations and public companies) would need knowledge of this section.

(a) RAISING CAPITAL AND DISPOSING OF PROFITS

The nationalized industries receive their finance from the government. In order to raise this capital the government may sell stocks in the nationalized industries on the Stock Exchange. These usually earn a fixed interest and can be bought by foreign firms and governments as well as British investors. Nationalized industries may also receive subsidies and grants from the government which will be financed out of taxation. Of course, if the nationalized industry makes a profit (as many do) then some of this may be 'ploughed back' into the industry. Profits may also be used to pay interest to stockholders or even be paid to the Chancellor of the Exchequer, thus leading to lower taxes.

(b) DO NATIONALIZED INDUSTRIES MAKE PROFITS?

Nationalized industries do not all make losses. However, there are industries such as British Steel and British Rail which tend to make losses more often than profits. On the other hand, they do provide employment for many workers, whilst other industries and areas of the country depend upon them. They are also engaged in providing a basic commodity or service essential to the nation as a whole.

Nationalized industries are increasingly under pressure from government to make profits. This may, however, be frustrated by other objectives of nationalized industries. These are:

(i) THE SOCIAL ROLE OF NATIONALIZED INDUSTRIES

This may require nationalized industries to provide unprofitable services because of public need. For example, an unprofitable power station or railway line may be vital to a small community in the Scottish Highlands.

(ii) THE GOVERNMENT HAS OTHER ECONOMIC OBJECTIVES

The nationalized industry may be prevented from increasing its prices because this may cause inflation. The industry may also be forced to buy British to 'prop up' another industry, even if it wished to purchase from elsewhere. An uneconomic coal mine may be kept open to prevent increased unemployment in regionally depressed areas such as South Wales.

Ideally, a nationalized industry should be left to be run by its managers. However, management can be obstructed by interference from the government, and this may harm its aim to make a profit.

(c) OWNERSHIP OF NATIONALIZED INDUSTRIES

Nationalized industries 'belong' to the government and people. They are organized and controlled, on behalf of the community, by the government through various boards and committees. Nationalized industries are government-owned industries.

(d) ORGANIZATION AND CONTROL

(i) ACT OF PARLIAMENT

Each nationalized industry is controlled by its Act of Parliament, which aims at setting up an organization most suited to that particular industry.

(ii) A MINISTER (A MEMBER OF THE GOVERNMENT)

The minister is appointed to control policy. He or she represents the public, is in charge of overall policy applying to the industry, and is subject to questions in Parliament.

(iii) A BOARD WILL BE APPOINTED BY THE MINISTER

The board has a chairman at its head. These boards are in charge of the day-to-day running of the industry. They are required to submit annual reports to Parliament and an annual debate normally takes place in Parliament to discuss the industry's affairs.

(iv) FINANCIAL AND STAFFING AFFAIRS

Boards are free from control but are expected to pay their way, taking one year with another. They employ their own staff and deal directly with trade unions over pay and conditions.

(v) CONSUMER PARTICIPATION

Consumers' councils have been set up to ensure direct consumer participation in the affairs of the nationalized industries. These consumer members are unpaid and nominated by bodies such as trade unions and local authorities. The councils deal with any complaints by and suggestions from consumers and advise both the boards and minister about consumer views.

Public accountability of the nationalized industries is achieved by the overall control of Parliament and consumer participation.

MC3 A public corporation comes into existence by means of
(*a*) registration under the Companies Acts
(*b*) a separate Act of Parliament for each one
(*c*) a Royal Charter
(*d*) a decision made by shareholders of the company concerned
(*e*) a national referendum

MC4 The members of the board of a public corporation are appointed by
(*a*) shareholders
(*b*) ratepayers
(*c*) a government minister
(*d*) the Registrar of Companies
(*e*) taxpayers

MC5 Nationalization is best defined as
(*a*) the acquisition by government of an industry to serve the interests of the nation as a whole
(*b*) the operation of private companies by government
(*c*) returning industries to the private enterprise sector
(*d*) converting public monopolies into private monopolies
(*e*) the government seizing control of foreign firms

4 LOCAL AUTHORITIES

We have so far considered the role and functions of public corporations which are activities controlled by central government. You should also be aware of the role and functions of local authorities.

(a) FUNCTIONS

Local authoirities consist of city councils and county councils, and for local affairs, borough and district councils. They have responsibility for essential services such as drainage, cleaning, street lighting, recreation, education, police, fire service and roads, etc.

(b) CONTROL

Control is exercised through a committee of council representatives (elected by local people) who in turn employ a full-time official to run affairs on a day-to-day basis. This person will be answerable to the committee for all matters affecting the local authority's undertakings.

(c) FINANCING

(i) ISSUING LOCAL GOVERNMENT STOCK

Local authorities issue stock through the Stock Exchange, borrow from the Public Works Loans Board at low interest rates and borrow from the banks. This provides capital to finance long-term expenditure such as new road construction or new school buildings.

(ii) SALE OF GOODS AND SERVICES

These include sea-front trading enterprises, entry fees to swimming pools and municipal golf courses and the hire of tennis courts in public parks. The idea is that those people who use these facilities should pay for or contribute to the cost of their upkeep.

(iii) CENTRAL GOVERNMENT GRANTS

Central government (Parliament in London) may make grants towards the cost of local authority spending. This is called the Rate Support Grant.

(iv) RATES

A rate is a tax levied by the local authority on the value of land and buildings. Each parcel of land and every building is given a 'rateable value' which is roughly equal to its annual letting value. The local authority calculates how much money it needs from the rates to support its expenditure, and will levy a rate of so many pence in the pound of rateable value, e.g. if the rateable value of a house is £1,000 and a rate of 20 pence in the pound is levied, then the householder's annual rate bill will be £200. Note: agricultural land is not subject to rates.

Advantages of rates
They provide a stable source of revenue from householders, industry and commerce.
It is difficult to avoid payment.
Wealthier home-owning citizens pay a higher contribution than those who do not own such property.

Disadvantages of rates
The ratepayer may never use many of the services, e.g. buses and recreational facilities.
Rates vary from area to area depending on the total spending of the

local authority and the number of householders, etc. who can contribute.

A householder's rates may increase if the property is improved (e.g. by adding a garage or central heating). This may discourage necessary improvements.

Rates are often criticized as an unsatisfactory method of raising revenue. Alternatives such as a local income tax, however, also have disadvantages. Nevertheless, reform of the rating system is expected in the not too distant future.

(d) THREE ALTERNATIVES TO RATES

(i) A LOCAL INCOME TAX

This could be collected either by the Inland Revenue (through PAYE – see p.186) or by the local authority.

There are problems with this system. If a firm's workforce comes from different local authority areas there will be different levels of local income tax to be paid and deducted by employers through PAYE. It will also add to the 'poverty trap' (see p.186), since it is equivalent to an increase in the basic rate of tax. It will discourage people from finding jobs. It will, however, be progressive (see p.184) for people who are unemployed or very low-income earners, unlike the present rating system.

(ii) A LOCAL SALES TAX

This may be a percentage tax in addition to VAT (see p.187) but would be levied only at the retail stage (unlike VAT, which is levied at all stages). The problems here include the fact that it may be regressive (see p.184) to someone who does not pay rates at the moment or who is a low income earner.

Another problem is that it will encourage cross-border shopping as consumers in high local sales tax areas got to shop in low local sales tax areas. This will lead to a waste of time and energy (petrol, etc.) for consumers and the revenues going to the local authority will be difficult to calculate. It will also lead to higher prices (inflation).

(iii) A POLL TAX

This would mean that every adult in a local authority would pay the same lump-sum amount of tax. It cannot be avoided but there may be exemptions, such as old people and people on social security. However, it can be regarded as regressive and households with many adults will pay more than they do under the present system.

MC6 The major source of capital for a nationalized industry is

(a)   the commercial bank
(b)   building societies
(c)   shareholders
(d)   overseas investors
(e)   taxpayers

MC7   One of the greatest problems of nationalized businesses is that
(a)   the government has no control
(b)   they cannot raise capital
(c)   they are always inefficient
(d)   they are too profitable
(e)   workers and managers often lack incentives

MC8   Which one of the following statements is an argument in favour of rates?
(a)   People who pay the highest rates use the local services more.
(b)   They ensure an equal level of income to local authorities throughout the country.
(c)   They provide local authorities with an independent source of revenue.
(d)   They are a progressive form of taxation.
(e)   They keep pace with inflation, as they increase with property values.

MC9   Local authorities derive income from all the following sources except
(a)   excise duties
(b)   rates
(c)   the money market
(d)   rate support grants
(e)   trading revenues

MC10   Which of the following organizations is found in the public sector of the UK economy?
(a)   public companies
(b)   unit trusts
(c)   co-operative societies
(d)   clearing banks
(e)   public corporations

5 PRIVATIZATION

In 1979 a Conservative government was elected, committed to reducing the size of the public sector. This policy included the privatization of many nationalized industries.

(a) PUBLICLY OWNED ASSETS WHICH HAVE BEEN SOLD OR ARE TO BE SOLD (AS AT SUMMER 1987)	*Already sold (in whole or part)* British Petroleum British Aerospace British Sugar Corporation Cable and Wireless Amersham International National Freight Corporation Britoil Associated British Ports Inter Aeradio British Rail Hotels Wytch Farm (British Gas) Enterprise Oil Sealink Jaguar British Technology Assets British Telecom British Airways National Bus Company Unipart Group of Companies British Gas Rolls-Royce	*To be sold* British Shipbuilders Electricity British Airports Authority British Steel Austin-Rover (formerly British Leyland) Water Authorities

(b) ARGUMENTS FOR PRIVATIZATION

(*i*)   These nationalized industries are returned to competitive market conditions and are driven by the profit motive. This leads to more efficiency. Public monopolies are destroyed.

(*ii*)   Management is freed from government interference in decision-making.

(*iii*)   As part of the private enterprise sector these industries are able to raise more finance from private investors.

(*iv*)   Trade unions have in the past treated nationalized industries as a 'soft touch' and have been able to operate restrictive practices (see p.137) and gain high wage increases.

(*v*)   The financial burden on the government is reduced. The government's public sector borrowing requirement (PSBR) can be made smaller. This means lower interest rates, as the government needs to borrow less. See pp.188–9 for an analysis of PSBR.

(*vi*)   The market mechanism is allowed to operate more freely to allocate resources.

(c) ARGUMENTS AGAINST PRIVATIZATION

The Labour Party has been opposed to the policy of privatization. Mr Kinnock has said, 'The British people's assets are being flogged off by the government.' The Labour Party is committed to re-nationalization.

(*i*)   Public monopolies are merely being replaced by private monopolies. Thus the problems with monopoly still applies – high prices for less variety and choice of product.
(*ii*)   Returning these industries to private enterprise may mean more unemployment as the industry is driven only by the profit motive.
(*iii*)   Only the profitable parts of the public sector will successfully be sold to private enterprise, e.g. British Telecom. However, how is the government going to sell the water authorities or Austin-Rover?
(*iv*)   The manner in which the nationalized industries have been sold. They have been sold too cheaply, allowing private investors large capital gains (e.g. British Telecom and Amersham International).

EXTENDED WRITING QUESTIONS

1 'It must be right to press ahead with the transfer of ownership from the state to private enterprise of as many public sector businesses as possible.'
(*a*)   What is meant by the public sector of the economy?
(*b*)   Why are some industries nationalized?
(*c*)   What are the arguments in favour of de-nationalization?
(*d*)   What arguments can be used against transferring the ownership of public enterprises to the private sector?

2 (*a*)   Explain the main differences between a public corporation and a plc in respect of:
            (i) ownership
            (ii) finance
            (iii) control
            (iv) objectives.
(*b*)   What are the main advantages of public corporations?
(*c*)   Should the size of a public corporation's surplus determine whether or not it has been successful?
(*d*)   What advantages might be expected if a previously nationalized industry is privatized?

3 Local authorities and public corporations are both part of public enterprise.
(*a*)   Name two services provided by local authorities.
(*b*)   State three sources of local authority revenue.
(*c*)   What is meant by the term public corporation?
(*d*)   How does a public corporation raise revenue?
(*e*)   Give three arguments for and against the privatization of a public corporation of your choice.

4 (*a*)   Describe the main features of a local authority revenue.
(*b*)   Why has there been public criticism about the way in which local people contribute through rates to the cost of local government services?
(*c*)   Discuss one alternative to rates (other than existing sources) as a source of revenue for local authorities.

5 (a)   Outline the main economic arguments in favour of nationalization.

(b)   What are the economic disadvantages of public ownership of industry?

(c)   How does a nationalized industry differ from a plc?

Answer

To answer (a) you need to discuss the advantages of nationalization.

They can: enjoy the economies of scale (tending to be large).

:   raise more capital and finance

:   operate more enterprises which could not (or should not) be provided by private enterprise.

:   operate those industries best operated on a national (rather than local) basis.

:   replace private monopolies.

:   prevent unemployment.

To answer (b) you need to discuss the disadvantages of nationalization (which is the public ownership of industry). Disadvantages include:

:   suffer the diseconomies of scale.

:   replace private monopolies with public monopolies (which are equally bad).

:   no profit motive, too much red tape (bureaucracy), too inflexible, slow to adapt and change.

:   they are inefficient and unprofitable.

To answer (c) you need to discuss the main differences between a Public Limited Company and a public corporation (nationalized industry). The plc is part of private enterprise and is purely motivated by profit. Public corporations are part of public enterprise and have a social role. Discuss the main differences regarding objectives; ownership and control; raising of finance and distribution of profits.

DATA RESPONSE   The Conservative government is committed to privatization of the nationalized industries in the UK. In 1986 it is proposed that British Gas be returned to the private sector.

(a)   Distinguish between the public sector and the private sector.

(b)   Name two previously nationalized industries which have been privatized.

(c)   Explain what is meant by the privatization of British Gas.

(d)   Analyse the likely consequences of the privatization of British Gas on

(i) gas prices for the consumer

(ii) ownership of the company

(iii) the raising of capital

(iv) the disposal of profits

(e)   Assess the arguments for and against the transfer of public assets such as British Gas to the private sector.

Answers to multiple-choice questions:

MC1	(*d*)		**MC6**	(*e*)
MC2	(*d*)		**MC7**	(*e*)
MC3	(*b*)		**MC8**	(*c*)
MC4	(*c*)		**MC9**	(*a*)
MC5	(*a*)		**MC10**	(*e*)

LABOUR

CONTENTS

This is a rather large chapter on all aspects of the labour force. The following topics are discussed:

1 **Labour as a factor of production** The quantity and quality of labour, mobility of labour: geographical and occupational. Productivity.

2 **Population** Factors determining the size of population, optimum population, the consequence of an increasing population, sex distribution of population, age distribution of population, geographical distribution of population, the working population.

3 **Wages** Terminology, methods of payment, different wages for different jobs, different wages within the same job. Equal pay. Income and wealth.

4 **Trade unions** Functions, types, organization, TUC, trades councils, Employers' association, the CBI, criticisms

1 LABOUR AS A FACTOR OF PRODUCTION

Labour is the human mental and physical effort involved in the production process. Labour – together with land, capital and enterprise – is a necessary factor input if production is to take place. The quality and quantity of a country's labour force will help to determine the quality and quantity of its national output of good and services.

(a) THE QUANTITY AND QUALITY OF LABOUR

(i) THE QUANTITY (SUPPLY) OF LABOUR DEPENDS ON:

– the size of the total population;
– the size of the working population, which is affected by many factors, discussed on p.127;
– the wage level – higher wages usually increases the number of hours people are prepared to work;
– the level of social benefits, which may discourage workers from offering themselves for employment;
– the length of the working week and the number of days' holiday.

(ii) THE QUALITY (EFFICIENCY) OF LABOUR DEPENDS ON:

- working conditions for the workers;
- education and training of workers;
- the quality of other factors of production with which labour works;
- the health of the labour force;
- incentives for workers.

(b) THE IMMOBILITY OF LABOUR

Labour as a factor of production is often said to be immobile. *Geographical* immobility refers to the reluctance of labour to move from region to region.

Occupational immobility describes reluctance or inability to move from job to job. Immobility of labour is a major factor associated with several types of unemployment discussed on pp.171–2.

(i) CAUSES OF GEOGRAPHICAL IMMOBILITY:

- Family and friendship ties in the area where the worker currently lives.
- Reluctance to disturb the children's education.
- Difficulties in obtaining accommodation, e.g. council house waiting lists or higher house prices in certain parts of the country.
- Natural fear of the unknown and ignorance of other areas.
- The financial cost of moving.
- Incomplete information about job opportunities.

(ii) CAUSES OF OCCUPATIONAL IMMOBILITY:

- Some jobs require long training periods.
- Some jobs require special qualifications or skills.
- Some jobs are dirty or dangerous.
- Lack of financial inducement to move jobs.
- The age of the worker.

The government, in its attempts to reduce unemployment, must reduce geographical and occupational immobility of labour. It attempts to overcome geographical immobility mainly by operating a regional policy to 'take the work to the workers'. (See pp.66–7.)

Geographical mobility could be encouraged by government grants for removal expenses, easier provision of accommodation and travel warrants for workers separated from their families.

Occupational immobility has been helped by government training centres and retraining schemes. Much of this is aimed at young people in the form of the Youth Training Scheme (YTS), which aims to train young unemployed persons. Occupational mobility would also be encouraged by a better flow of information concerning jobs.

(c) PRODUCTIVITY

This is a measure of output flowing from the use of given amounts of factors of production. Labour productivity is usually expressed as the number of units of output produced per person per unit of time (i.e. output per worker).

A high level of productivity indicates efficiency and is regarded as a significant factor in the achievement of economic growth (see p.155) and a high standard of living. Indeed, the UK's disappointing economic growth record throughout the 1960s and 1970s is often blamed on poor levels of labour productivity.

There are several factors which influence a higher level of labour productivity:

(i)   The use of more and better capital equipment will increase labour productivity. Replacing old and out-of-date equipment.

(ii)   Improvements in organization such as more division of labour and the achievement of economies of large-scale production.

(iii)   Better-quality labour force with better skills and better education.

(iv)   Concentrating production on those firms and industries which are expanding and already achieving growth. This should be combined with a contraction of those industries now in decline, overmanned and unproductive.

(v)   Government policies aimed at achieving all the above, i.e. to encourage investment in growth section of the economy and train people in skills which are required.

2 POPULATION

(a) THE SIZE OF POPULATION

In 1985 the population of the UK was 56.4 million, which makes it the world's fifteenth largest.

	Surface area (square km)	Population (millions)	Population density per sq km
England	130.439	46.8	359
Wales	20.768	2.8	135
Scotland	78.777	5.2	66
Northern Ireland	14.120	1.6	113
United Kingdom	244.100	56.4	231

Three main factors determine the size of a country's population: death rate, birth rate and migration.

(i) DEATH RATE

Death rate is the number of death per thousand of population in a given year. In 1983, the death rate for the UK was around 11.8 and has remained fairly static over many years. As death rate falls, so the average age to which people live increases. In 1983 life expectancy was seventy years for a male and seventy-six for a female.

Factors which have led to a fall in the death rate include:
– better medical knowledge and more health care;
– better food, shelter and clothing;
– better-educated population concerned with health and fitness;
– better conditions at work;
– better sanitation;
– the decline in the infant mortality rate due to better antenatal and postnatal care, standard of living improvements and improved medical care facilities. Infant mortality has dropped from 142 per thousand live births in 1900 to 10.1 per thousand live births in 1983.

(ii) BIRTH RATE

The birth rate is the number of births per thousand of population in a given year. In 1983 the birth rate was 12.8 (in 1971 it was 16.1) and the general trend since 1900 has been for a decline in the birth rate. The birth rate depends on:
– the use of birth control and abortion techniques, which may be influenced by moral and religious views;
– ideas of family size, which are determined by factors such as hoped-for standard of living, availability of child benefits and the role of women;
– the number of marriages. Most children are born to married couples. The age of marriage (especially for the woman) will be significant, as will the divorce rate and, again, the role of women.

Why do you think there has been a trend in the UK for a decline in the birth rate?

If the birth rate is greater than the death rate, which it normally is, then this is termed a *natural increase in population*. If the birth rate is lower than the death rate, this is a *natural decrease in population*.

(iii) MIGRATION

Migration is a significant factor determining the size of population. Net emigration means that more people emigrate (leave) than immigrate (arrive). Net immigration means that more people immigrate than emigrate.

In the UK in the decade before 1983 net emigration amounted to 365,000 people. In the last thirty years, UK citizens have tended to emigrate to countries such as Australia, New Zealand, Canada and the USA. People immigrating to the UK come mainly from India, Pakistan and the West Indies.

The population of the UK is now fairly static. It increased by 10 per cent between 1951 and 1971, and has increased only slightly since 1971.

| (b) OPTIMUM POPULATION | Optimum population is that level of population needed to maximize the use of available resources (land, labour, capital and enterprise). It is the most efficient level of population, where national income per head is maximized (see p.154). |

Optimum population is that level of population needed to maximize the use of available resources (land, labour, capital and enterprise). It is the most efficient level of population, where national income per head is maximized (see p.154).

If a country is overpopulated, resources are insufficient to meet the demands on them, as illustrated in less developed countries. National income per head will be very low. If a country is underpopulated, resources are not being used enough and are being wasted. National income per head will be lower than it should be

A change in the state of technology will affect the size of optimum population because resources may be more efficiently used even without population changes.

(c) INCREASING POPULATION

(i) THE ADVANTAGES OF INCREASING POPULATION

–   If the population is below the optimum size, an increase in population will lead to a better use of resources and increase national income per head.

–   If the increase in population is due to a higher birth rate, more young people will lead to a more flexible and adventurous attitude in the population.

–   There will be more demand in the economy, leading to an increase in output, more jobs and more specialization and economies of scale.

(ii) THE DISADVANTAGES OF AN INCREASING POPULATION

–   If the increase in population results in a population larger than optimum population, there will be a strain on existing resources and national income per head will fall.

–   If the increase in population is due to a lower death rate, more old people will put a strain on the taxpayer to support them with pensions, old people's homes, etc. Older people also tend to be more conservative and less flexible.

–   The country may have to import more food and raw materials, which may worsen the balance of payments

–   There will be more demand for services like education, health and roads, etc. There will be an increased burden on the taxpayer.

(d) THE SEX DISTRIBUTION OF POPULATION

In the UK population as a whole there are more females than males. Up to the age of fifty, however, there are more males than females. In the older age groups the number of females is greater than that of males, and this pattern intensifies in the really old groups.

There are more males in the younger age groups because there are more male births and the decline in infant mortality has had very beneficial effects on males, who tend to be weaker when very young.

In the older age groups there are more females because the death rate amongst males in *all* age groups is greater. Also women live longer than men, perhaps because they smoke and drink less, do less dangerous work and are physically and mentally stronger. (What do you think?) Moreover, the older age groups are those who fought in two world wars, where proportionately a much greater number of males died.

In 1983 there were 28.9 million females and 27.5 million males in the UK.

(e) THE AGE DISTRIBUTION OF POPULATION

In 1983 the age distribution of population in the UK was:

0–15 years	:	11.1 million
16–64 years	:	36.9 million
65+ years	:	8.4 million

The under-sixteens are a declining proportion of the UK population, whereas those over sixty-five are a growing population.

The UK has an ageing population and the average age is increasing. This is due to a fall in the birth rate and a fall in the death rate.

The consequences of an ageing population include:

(i) changes in demand patterns, as there is an increase in demand for commodities required by old people and less demand for those commodities required by young persons and babies.

(ii) a less flexible and less adventurous population. Older people are more conservative and set in their ways.

(iii) an increased burden on the population to produce the goods and services and provide the taxation to support the older groups. The old need more money spent on them in the form of pensions, old people's homes and health care.

(iv) older people are less geographically and occupationally mobile (see p.122).

(f) THE GEOGRAPHICAL DISTRIBUTION OF POPULATION

There are a number of significant points to make about where the UK's population live, i.e. the geographical distribution of population:

(i) The majority of people live in the South-East and Midlands of England. The South-East of England is where most industry is located and where the jobs are.

(ii) The majority of people live in cities (urban areas). London has a population of approximately 8 million. There seven large conurbations (i.e. towns and cities merged to form one big urban area), including Merseyside, the West Midlands and Glasgow. Traditionally, jobs are to be found in the cities.

(iii) There has been an expansion of population in towns like Telford, Welwyn Garden City and Milton Keynes. This has coincided with a decline in population in the inner-city areas of the large cities, where the housing is old and there are few services.

(iv) There is a high proportion of older people in south coast towns such as Eastbourne and Worthing. Many older people move south because of the milder climate. The high proportion of old people puts a strain on the rates in these towns.

(g) THE WORKING POPULATION

(i) WHAT IS THE WORKING POPULATION?

The working population consists of all those people over the age of sixteen who are either in employment or actively seeking employment (i.e. registered as unemployed).

It includes:
– people in paid employment, even if they are over the retirement age (sixty-five for men, sixty for women)
– part-time workers
– self-employed workers
– members of the armed forces.

It does not include:
– children under sixteen
– students involved in full-time education
– housepersons not seeking work
– prisoners
– people who are physically or mentally incapable of work
– people living on private income.

The size of the working population can be altered by changes in the school-leaving age, retirement age and numbers of housepersons seeking work. In 1984 the size of the working population was 28,061,000 people, which is 48 per cent of the total population.

(ii) THE IMPORTANCE OF THE WORKING POPULATION

The working population is important because it provides the tax revenue and produces the goods and services required by other groups in society. The *dependent population* (i.e. very old and young people) is so called because it is dependent on the working population.

(iii) THE OCCUPATIONAL DISTRIBUTION OF THE WORKING POPULATION

The economy is divided into three broad sections: the primary sector, secondary sector and tertiary sector. You should now refer to pp.55–6 for a discussion of the meaning of these terms. In your reading you should establish that the long-term trend is towards expansion of the tertiary sector and decline of the primary and secondary sectors. Why should this be so? In the last ten years or so, however, the primary sector has expanded. Why? Pages 55–6 will provide the answers to these questions.

(iv) THE ROLE OF WORKING WOMEN

The long-term trend is towards more and more women looking for employment. This trend involves married as well as single women. The reasons for this include:
– smaller family size;
– many families desiring a better standard of living, which needs more income into the household;
– labour-saving devices (e.g. washing machines, dishwashers), which have given women more time for alternative activities;
– the changing role of women in society as a whole – women are no longer barred from certain jobs and activities;
– government legislation encouraging equal pay and discouraging sex discrimination in jobs.
   The increasing work role of women is having important consequences for our economy and society. Make a list of some of these consequences.

MC1 Which of the following will increase the size of a country's working population?
(a)   an increase in the number of emigrants
(b)   raising the school-leaving age
(c)   raising the retirement age
(d)   a reduction in the numbers of unemployed
(e)   an increase in the birth rate

MC2 A natural increase of the population means:
(a)   infant mortality rate is declining
(b)   immigration exceeds emigration
(c)   total population size is greater than the optimum size
(d)   death rate is less than birth rate
(e)   birth rate is less than death rate

MC3 Which of the following would *not* lead to an increase in the size of population?
(a)   improved methods of contraception
(b)   lower levels of infant mortality

(c)   a fall in the death rate
(d)   immigration exceeds emigration
(e)   death rate is less than birth rate

MC4 A fall in the death rate is likely to result in which of the following?
(a)   an increase in the geographical mobility of labour
(b)   an increase in government spending on old age pensions
(c)   no effect on consumer spending patterns
(d)   reduced spending in the health service
(e)   a reduced level of national income

MC5 Optimum population is defined by the economist as the level of population at which
(a)   productivity is maximized
(b)   death rate equals birth rate
(c)   emigration equals immigration
(d)   national income is maximized
(e)   national income per head is maximized

3 WAGES

Wages is a broad term meaning the reward (or income) going to the factor of production labour.

(a) TERMINOLOGY OF WAGES

(i) Wage rates . . . wages are the payment for a job measured in units of time or pieces of work. Wages tend to be paid weekly and in the form of cash.

(ii) Salaries . . . tend to be paid monthly and in the form of cheques. The salary will remain fixed, irrespective of the actual length of time worked or pieces of work produced.

(iii) Earnings . . . the total money earned which includes the basic wage, overtime and bonuses. Earnings are gross wages.

(iv) Take-home pay . . . is the net wage which the person actually has to spend after tax, national insurance and other stoppages have been deleted. This is sometimes called disposable wages (or income).

(v) Money wages . . . wages in money terms.

(vi) Real wages . . . money wages in terms of the goods and services which can be bought. Real wages take into account the cost of living (inflation).

(vii) **Perks and fringe benefits** . . . include a range of non-monetary pay-ments such as low-cost mortgages, the company car and private health schemes.

(b) METHODS OF PAYMENT

Pay is usually calculated in one of two ways: time rates and piece rates.

(i) TIME RATES

Wages are paid per unit of time worked. All workers doing the same work receive the same wage. This method usually operates when the work output cannot be measured (e.g. nurses), when the quality of work done is more important than the quantity, and when there is no link between effort and pay. Usually workers have to 'clock in' and 'clock out' of work.

(ii) PIECE RATES

Wages are linked to the number of units produced. This is an incentive to workers to produce as many units as possible, and they can check that they have received the correct wage. However, piece rates may lead to more quantity but less quality. Quality inspectors may be required, and not all jobs lend themselves to piece rates (e.g. teaching).

(c) DIFFERENT WAGES FOR DIFFERENT JOBS

Wages differ between different occupations. Doctors earn more than shop assistants, footballers generally earn more than refuse collec-tors. The main influence on wages paid in a particular occupation is the interaction of demand for labour and the supply of labour avail-able to do the job. The greater the demand and the less the supply of labour, the higher will be wages.

(i) FACTORS INFLUENCING THE DEMAND FOR LABOUR

Labour is a derived demand, therefore changes in the demand for a product caused by successful advertising or changes in taste will affect the demand for labour to produce the product.

The marginal revenue product of workers

marginal product = the increase in total output brought about by employing one more worker. Refer to pp.59–60 on the law of eventually diminishing returns.

marginal revenue product = marginal product × the price of the finished good.

Labour will be employed up to the point where MRP = wages.

Let us refer to this table to illustrate this *marginal productivity theory of wages*. Let us assume that the price of potatoes is £2 per kilogram.

No. of people employed	Marginal product of potatoes (kg)	Marginal revenue product (Marginal product × price)
1	2	4
2	14	28
3	38	76
4	25	50
5	15	30
6	13	26
7	12	24
8	10	20

Here, at a wage of £50, the farmer would employ four people because £50 equals the MRP £50. Thus the higher is a worker's MRP, the higher will be the wage he/she receives.

Problems with the Marginal Productivity Theory
Not all workers have a marginal product which can be measured easily (e.g. teachers, nurses).

It is too simple to assume that all units of labour are identical and that they use the same machinery, etc.

If demand for labour is inelastic, wages will be high. Demand for labour is likely to be more inelastic if labour cannot be replaced by machinery, the demand for the finished good is inelastic and if wages are only a small proportion of total costs.

(ii) FACTORS INFLUENCING THE SUPPLY OF LABOUR

– Special skills and abilities may be required – if so, supply may be restricted (e.g. footballers).
– Special qualifications may be required (e.g. doctors).
– A trade union may be operating a 'closed shop' (see p.137).
– The job may be dirty or dangerous.

(d) DIFFERENT WAGES WITHIN THE SAME JOB

Even within the same occupation some people may receive higher wages than others; e.g. some teachers may earn more than other teachers. There may be several reasons for this:
(i) Some people have received promotion within the job – they receive higher wages for more responsibility.

(ii)　　Some people receive perks and fringe benefits (e.g. a company car).

(iii)　　Some people have been longer in the job and received annual incremental rises in wages.

(iv)　　Women still receive less than men in many jobs.

(v)　　People who work in and around London receive higher wages because of the higher cost of living (e.g. house prices).

(e) EQUAL PAY

During the 1970s there were three main Acts of Parliament aimed at achieving equal pay for women. The Equal Pay Act 1970 required that women should be paid the same as men for similar work. The Sex Discrimination Act 1976 required that women should not be discriminated against in employment opportunities. The Employment Protection Act 1978 laid down some provisions for payment and job protection for a woman having a baby. However, despite this legislation, women are still paid less than men. Possible reasons sometimes put forward, many of which you may disagree with, include:

(i)　　Women workers tend to be younger on average than men.

(ii)　　Women are able to do fewer jobs than men.

(iii)　　Women's promotion prospects are badly affected by child-bearing.

(iv)　　Women are believed to have a higher absence rate.

(v)　　Married women do not work as hard, relying primarily on the husband's income.

(vi)　　Women tend to do less well-paid, unskilled work.

(vii)　　Women have fewer academic qualifications.

(viii)　　Male employers are still prejudiced against women.

(ix)　　Trade unions with a high proportion of female members tend to be weak (e.g. nurses, teachers).

The equal pay legislation, although largely ineffectual, may have had some effects:

(i)　　More women at work, improving the standard of living for many families.

(ii)　　A further decline in the birth rate.

(iii)　　An increase in male unemployment because women tend to accept lower wages.

(iv)　　More women trade unionists.

(v)　　Greater public acceptance about issues such as equal pay and women's role in society and the economy.

(f) INCOME AND WEALTH

(i) DISTINGUISHING BETWEEN INCOME AND WEALTH

Income is a *flow* of money going to a factor of production (or the owner of a factor of production) over some specified period of time. The flow of income to the factor of production, labour, is termed wages

Wealth is a *stock* of assets, which have a market value, at any one moment of time. The ownership of wealth can generate income. Wealth may include the ownership of a house, stocks and shares, consumer goods and capital goods.

Capital is that form of wealth which contributes to production, e.g. factories and machines (commonly known as capital goods).

(ii) THE CREATION OF INCOME AND WEALTH

Incomes are created by the factor of production, or its owner, hiring out the factor in return for a flow of income, e.g. a labourer hires out his labour for a wage.

The creation of wealth occurs when value is added to inputs of materials by an economic activity. The production process generates wealth because value is added to materials and other inputs during the process. Thus any manufacturing or service industry contributes to wealth creation. Specialization (division of labour) is also a significant factor contributing to wealth creation.

(iii) THE DISTRIBUTION OF INCOME AND WEALTH

The distribution of income within the UK is unequal. In 1983 25 per cent of the total pre-tax income earned went to the top 10 per cent of income earners. The bottom 10 per cent of income earners accounted for only 2.3 per cent of total income earned. This means that high-income earners, although relatively few in number, account for a large proportion of total income.

The distribution of wealth is also unequal in the UK. For instance, two-thirds of personal wealth is owned by only 10 per cent of the adult population, half of all personal wealth is owned by 5 per cent of the adult population, and a quarter of all personal wealth is owned by 1 per cent of the adult population.

This represents a more unequal distribution of wealth than other Western European countries.

(iv) FACTORS INFLUENCING THE DISTRIBUTION OF INCOME AND WEALTH

Income distribution is influenced by:
– distribution of wealth ownership. Since wealth generates income, the more wealth an individual owns, the more income is generated.
– fiscal policy – a progressive tax system, e.g. income tax, and government spending on transfer payments (i.e. pensions, social security and unemployment benefits) will reduce the unequal income distribution. See pp.184–5.
– wage differences between occupations. Some jobs award higher wages than others. The reasons for this were discussed on pp.130–1.

Wealth distribution is influenced by:

–   the historical accumulation of wealth and inheritance.
–   fiscal policy – a progressive tax system, e.g. inheritance tax and even wealth tax, would redistribute wealth from rich to poor. Government spending on transfer payments and social capital (schools, hospitals, old people's homes) would also redistribute wealth.
–   incomes – a more equal distribution of income would mean that wealth accumulation would become equal.

MC6   Which of the following is likely to hinder rises in the wage rate in a particular industry?
(*a*)   an increase in demand for the industry's product
(*b*)   a fall in the price of a close substitute
(*c*)   wages are a low proportion of the industry's total costs
(*d*)   machines cannot do the work performed by labour
(*e*)   a rise in the profits made by the industry

MC7   Shop assistants are relatively poorly paid. This is best explained by the fact that:
(*a*)   the work is unpleasant
(*b*)   the work is repetitive
(*c*)   the work is tiring
(*d*)   the work is unskilled
(*e*)   the work is boring

MC8   Which of the following would give greater power to labour to achieve a wage rise?
(*a*)   the final product has a high elasticity of demand
(*b*)   the selling price of the final product is low
(*c*)   labour cannot be easily substituted by capital
(*d*)   wages are high proportion of total costs
(*e*)   the work is unskilled

MC9   Real income can be defined as:
(*a*)   take-home pay (i.e. disposable income)
(*b*)   income in terms of its purchasing power
(*c*)   wages plus overtime
(*d*)   all earned and unearned income
(*e*)   wages in money terms

4 TRADE UNIONS

Trade unions represent about half the British working population. British trade unions are dominated by fewer, but bigger unions such as the Transport and General Workers Union (TGWU).

(a) THE FUNCTIONS OF TRADE UNIONS	**(i) To further their members' interests** To improve pay and working conditions, to protect jobs and to protect workers from the abuse of management power.
	(ii) To improve conditions throughout society e.g. education, pensions and the welfare state.
	(iii) To improve economic prosperity throughout the country e.g. to encourage economic growth, reduce inflation and unemployment.
	(iv) To participate in national politics Most trade unions support the Labour Party both financially and philosophically.
(b) TYPES OF TRADE UNION	**(i) Craft unions** The oldest type of union. They tend to represent skilled workers from various industries and to be quite small, e.g. Electricians' Union.
	(ii) Industrial unions These unions include both skilled and unskilled workers from a specific industry, e.g. National Union of Mineworkers (NUM).
	(iii) General unions These unions include members from a variety of industries doing a variety of skilled and unskilled work. Some general unions are very large; the TGWU, for example, has a membership of approximately 2 million.
	(iv) White-collar unions These unions represent non-manual workers who usually work in an office. These are expanding, e.g. National And Local Government Officers Association (NALGO).
(c) THE ORGANIZATION OF A TRADE UNION	Although unions have a separate existence, there are some common features:
	(i) The membership . . . the workers who pay their subscription to the union.
	(ii) Shop stewards . . . elected representatives of the membership who carry out day-to-day activities at the workplace.
	(iii) The branch . . . the local branch admits new members, elects delegates to conference, elects local officers and discusses national and local agreements.
	(iv) Full-time officials . . . full-time workers for the union who represent

the membership in a range of firms. They help the branches and shop stewards.

(v) The national executive . . . a group of people elected by the membership to carry out national union policy. They are the leadership of the union.

(vi) The General Secretary . . . the most important full-time official, who is responsible for the day-to day running of the union throughout the country. The General Secretary is elected by the union membership.

(vii) The Conference . . . an assembly of representatives of the membership from the branches. The conference meets once a year and is the policy-making body of the union.

(d) THE TUC, TRADES COUNCILS, EMPLOYERS' ASSOCIATIONS AND THE CBI

(i) The TUC . . . the central body of the union movement. Most trade unions belong to the TUC, which represents the union movement on national issues (e.g. discussions with government). It is headed by a General Secretary.

(ii) Trades councils . . . local meetings of delegates from different trade unions.

(iii) Employers' federations or associations . . . include employers from specific industries to discuss matters concerning their industry.

(iv) The Confederation of British Industry (CBI) . . . represents employers from a variety of industries in national discussions with government and the TUC. It is headed by a Director-General.

(e) CRITICISMS OF TRADE UNIONS

Trade unions have been criticized for certain aspects of their behaviour. Indeed, legislation has been passed by the Conservative governments of Mrs Thatcher to curtail trade-union power. The main legislation is the Employment Act 1980. Criticism of trade unions includes:

(i) INDUSTRIAL DISPUTES

Trade unions are accused of taking industrial action, which causes much economic damage and disruption. There are several forms of action: work-to-rule, go-slow, overtime ban and strike. Strikes are of two main types
- *Official strikes* . . . recognized and supported by the union.
- *Unofficial strikes* . . . usually local and called by a shop steward without the recognition of the union (which may come later).

(ii) USE OF RESTRICTIVE PRACTICES

There are several main types:

Closed shops All workers have to be in the trade union. This is seen to be against individual liberty.

Restricting labour supply Workers may have to serve abnormally long apprenticeships. This reduces the supply of labour and keeps wages high.

Demarcation disputes Only certain workers from a specific union can do a particular job (however small).

Other restrictive practices Refusal to operate new technology, time-wasting, unnecessary overtime and kangaroo courts of discipline.

(iii) PICKETING

When a strike is called, pickets aim to persuade all workers not to attend work. They do this by forming a picket line outside the place of work. Pickets are accused of sometimes being too violent and picketing of the firm's suppliers (known as secondary picketing) spread the disruption.

(iv) UNION DEMOCRACY

Unions are sometimes accused of being undemocratic because:
–   Many do not use secret ballots, which leads to intimidation.
–   Branches are dominated by activists.
–   Card votes represent many votes at conference.
–   There is a show of hands to gauge members' views.
–   They operate closed shops.

(v) THERE ARE TOO MANY TRADE UNIONS

This makes negotiations difficult for firms.

(vi) TRADE UNIONS DO NOT TAKE INTO ACCOUNT THE WIDER INTEREST OF THE COUNTRY AS A WHOLE

Trade unions act only in the interest of their members. Critics would argue that they are too bound by history and tradition and do not look forward enough. They are interested primarily in wages and ignore their other objectives.

MC10   Which of the following is an industrial union?
(*a*)   GMWU (municipal workers)

(b) APEX (clerks)
(c) SOGAT (printers)
(d) BMA (doctors)
(e) NUM (miners)

EXTENDED WRITING QUESTIONS

1 (a) What important information is discovered by a population census?
(b) Distinguish between
(i) death rate
(ii) infant mortality rate
(iii) natural increase in population.
(c) Give three likely reasons for a decrease in the UK birth rate.
(d) Outline the economic effects of a rise in the average of population in the UK.

Answer

(a) The collection of information is much more than a head count. A census gives the following information about present population (and allows for future projections):
– size of population; age, sex and geographical distribution of population.
  It allows for government to plan how many schools to build, where to build schools, what services to provide for the elderly, how many people will be entering/leaving the labour force.
  The census is essential for government decision-making. The census also gives valuable social information such as numbers of divorces, separations, occupational and educational backgrounds, number of people per household.
(b) Death rate is the number of people who die per thousand of population in one year in one country. Infant mortality rate is the number of deaths of infants under one year per 1,000 live births in a year. The natural increase in population is the difference betwen the number of births and the number of deaths in one year in a country. A natural increase occurs when the number of births is greater than the number of deaths.
(c) Three factors from the following:
(i) Better and more widely used birth-control methods.
(ii) Ideas of family size change to smaller families with fewer children.
(iii) Fewer women of child-bearing age.
(iv) Women staying at work longer to have a career and earn their own income.
(d) – Much depends on whether the optimum level of population has already been reached. If the population is more than the optimum, living standards will fall as resources are even more thinly spread. If the population is below optimum, the

increasing population will increase living standards as better use is made of resources.

– The aggregate level of demand should also rise for all goods and services.

– Finally, much depends on which age group forms the increasing population. More babies in the population will change consumption patterns, as will more old people. There may be a greater dependent population and consequently a greater burden on the working population.

2 (*a*) Distinguish between geographical mobility of labour and geographical distribution of labour.

(*b*) Describe and account for changes in
(i) geographical distribution of population
(ii) occupational distribution of population within the UK since 1945.

(*c*) What changes do you anticipate in the occupational distribution in the UK during the next ten years? Give reasons for your answer.

3 A manufacturing company employs both skilled and unskilled women. Some of the skilled workers have taken *unofficial industrial action*, claiming that their *differentials have been eroded*. They are also unhappy because management have refused to accept a *closed shop*.

(*a*) What is meant by the phrases in italics in the passage?

(*b*) To what type of union are (i) the unskilled and (ii) the skilled worker likely to belong?

(*c*) Give two advantages of a closed shop.

(*d*) Describe the role of the shop steward.

(*e*) Explain three problems which might arise if there are several unions in existence within the factory.

4 The number of workers prepared to work for a firm at different hourly wage rates varies as follows:

Hourly wage	£4.00	£5.00	£6.00	£7.00	£8.00
Number of workers	100	200	300	400	600

(*a*) (i) On graph paper draw the supply curve for labour; label it S1.

(ii) From your answer to (1) estimate how many workers would accept employment for £4.80.

(iii) Assume that the supply of labour was totally fixed at 350 and would not increase or decrease no matter what wage was offered. Draw a curve on the graph paper to illustrate this. Label it S2.

(*b*) What factors determine the incomes of famous pop stars?

5 (*a*)   Distinguish between (i) time rates and (ii) piece rates as methods of payment.

(*b*)   What is diminishing marginal productivity? Give an arithmetical example.

(*c*)   Why do First Division footballers earn more than nurses?

DATA RESPONSE

After increasing by about one-tenth between 1951 and 1971, the population of the UK has become almost stationary. It rose by only 0.5 per cent between 1971 and 1976, remained static until 1980 and has since risen slightly.

The *birth rate* has fallen from 16.1 in 1971 to 12.8 in 1983, while the *death rate* has remained virtually unchanged at around 11.8. In 1983 there were 659,000 deaths and 694,000 live births. The number of births, after falling steadily from 980,000 in 1964 to 632,000 in 1977, rose to 725,000 in 1980 and has since fallen by 4 per cent. Some common causes of death in 1983 were heart disease (216,542), cancer (148,647), respiratory diseases (93,886), and road accidents (5,790).

In the decade to 1983, the population of the UK was reduced by about 365,000 through *net migration*.

Life expectancy at birth is about 70 years for males and 76 for females.

Infant mortality in 1983 was 10.1, slightly less than in the USA, but higher than in other comparable countries, such as Japan (6.2), Denmark (8.0) and France (8.9). (Source: *Britain An Economic Profile* (Lloyds Bank))

(*a*)   Explain the meaning of the italicized words in the passage.

(*b*)   What was the natural increase in population in 1983?

(*c*)   (i) What factors determine the size of population?
(ii) With reference to the UK, explain what has happened to these factors since the early 1970s.

(*d*)   What might be the economic consequences of an increasing population?

(*e*)   Briefly distinguish between
(i) occupational distribution of population
(ii) geographical distribution of population
(iii) age distribution of population.

(*f*)   Give three reasons why people are living longer in the 1980s than in previous decades?

(*g*)   Give three consequences of an ageing population.

Answers to multiple-choice questions:

MC1	*(c)*	**MC6**	*(b)*
MC2	*(d)*	**MC7**	*(d)*
MC3	*(a)*	**MC8**	*(c)*
MC4	*(b)*	**MC9**	*(b)*
MC5	*(e)*	**MC10**	*(e)*

THE CIRCULAR FLOW, NATIONAL INCOME AND ECONOMIC GROWTH

CONTENTS

This chapter is concerned with national income. The chapter has been subdivided into the following topics:

1   **Factors determining a nation's income and output**
    The meaning and importance of national income.
    The circular flow in a simple, closed and open economy.
    The main components of aggregate demand:
    Consumption.
    Savings.
    Investment.

2   **Measurement of national income**
    Output, expenditure and income methods of measurement.
    Difficulties in measuring the national income.
    Uses of national income statistics.
    Economic growth.

1 FACTORS DETERMINING A NATION'S INCOME AND OUTPUT

(a) THE MEANING AND IMPORTANCE OF NATIONAL INCOME

The national income (Y) is the money value of all goods and services produced in an economy in a particular period of time (usually one year).

The size of Y in a country is very important because it influences the level of employment, the level of output and people's standard of living. Usually an increase in Y will mean more jobs, more output and a better standard of living. A fall in Y will have the opposite effect.

Y is determined by the *total level (or aggregate) demand* in the economy (AD). An economy is in *equilibrium* (i.e. all opposing forces in balance and all things remaining equal, there is no need to change) when:

$$Y = AD$$

This is when the supply (or output) of goods and services produced in the economy is equal to the demand for these goods and services. If AD is greater than Y, Y will have to rise. If Y is greater than AD, Y will have to fall. The economy will eventually have to end up at equilibrium.

(b) THE CIRCULAR FLOW

(i) THE CIRCULAR FLOW OF INCOME IN A SIMPLE ECONOMY WHERE ALL INCOME IS CONSUMED

The operation of forces in an economy can be expressed in the form of a circular flow of incomes and spending between households and firms. A household is a group of people (consumers) earning incomes and spending them on goods and services produced by the firms. In this simple economy we assume that the household spends all income. This spending on consumer goods (termed consumption (C)) is the only component of AD in this simple economy.

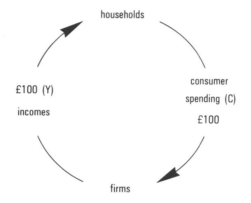

This economy is in equilibrium because: Y = AD

$$Y = C$$

If Y was greater than C, Y would fall; if Y was less than C, Y would rise.

(ii) THE CIRCULAR FLOW OF INCOME IN A CLOSED ECONOMY

A closed economy exists when there is no international trade. We shall also assume that in this particular closed economy there is no government spending or taxation. Here households have two alternative used for their income – they can consume it or they can *save it*. Savings are (S). AD consists of C and S.

S are lost to Y and will reduce the level of Y. However, some (if not all) of S will be used to finance *investment* (I). I is the creation of real capital goods such as machinery and factories, and adds to Y. If S = I, then the Y is in equilibrium.

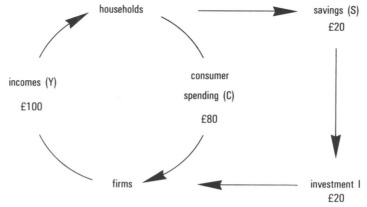

In this economy:

$$Y = AD$$
Therefore $Y = C + I$
In equilibrium $S = I$

However, if S is greater than I, AD and Y will fall. If I is greater than S, AD and Y will rise.

(iii) THE CIRCULAR FLOW OF INCOME IN AN OPEN ECONOMY

An open economy is one in which international trade exists. Assume also that there is government spending and taxation.

Thus households need not consume all of their income. Some may be saved (S), spent on imports (M), or taxed (T). S, and M and T are known as withdrawals (W) or leakages. An increase in W will reduce the level of Y.

However, Y will be added to by investment (I), government spending (G) and money spent by foreigners on exports (X). These are known as injections (J).

In an open economy the size of Y is determined by the size of AD, which is determined by C + I + G + X.

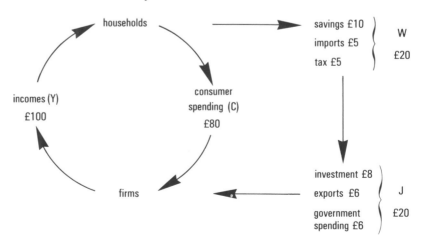

In this economy:
$$Y = AD$$
Therefore
$$Y = C + I + G + X$$
$$= C + J$$

In equilibrium, J = W. If J was greater than W, Y would rise. If W was greater than J, Y would fall.

(c) THE MAIN COMPONENTS OF AD

Let us look in more detail at the main components determining AD. These are consumption (C), investment (I) and savings (S). Government spending (G) and taxation (T) are discussed in detail in Chapter 9. Exports (X) and imports (M) are discussed in detail in Chapter 11.

(d) CONSUMPTION (C)

Consumption is consumer spending (or expenditure). This is the biggest component of AD and therefore the biggest determinant of the size of Y. C is spending on domestically produced goods and services. There is a direct relationship between C and Y – as C increases, so does Y (and vice versa).

DETERMINANTS OF C

(i) THE SIZE OF INCOME As Y rises, so will C. However, the relationship between C and Y is not so clear-cut. An increase in Y will cause C to increase by a proportionately lower amount. The proportion of an increase in Y which is C is termed the *marginal propensity to consume* (MPC). MPC will fall as a country's (or individual's) Y increases. The average proportion of Y which is consumed is termed the *average propensity to consume* (APC), and this also declines as Y increases.

$$MPC = \frac{Change\ in\ C}{Change\ in\ Y} \qquad APC = \frac{C}{Y}$$

(ii) The distribution of income High-income consumers spend more than low-income consumers. However, MPC and APC both decline as Y increases. A redistribution of Y from high-income to low-income consumers will increase C.

(iii) Cost of credit High interest rates on loans will reduce the level of C.

(iv) Availability of credit If credit is generally available from banks and hire purchase companies, the level of C will rise.

(v) Government policy Government fiscal policy will affect C. If the government operates a progressive tax system and spends money on welfare payments to the poor, C will increase. This is because low-income earners have a high MPC.

(e) SAVINGS

Savings is a withdrawal from Y, and an increase in S will reduce the size of Y. S is that part of Y, in a closed economy, which is not spent on C. S includes buying securities and depositing money with financial institutions (banks, building societies, etc.).

Determinants of S

(i) **The size of income** As Y rises, so will S. However, as with C, the relationship between Y and S is not clear-cut. An increase in Y will cause S to increase by a proportionately greater amount. The proportion of an increase in Y which is saved is termed the *Marginal Propensity to Save* (MPS). MPS will rise as a country's (or individual's) Y increases. The average proportion of Y which is saved is termed the *average propensity to save* (APS), and this also rises as Y rises.

$$MPS = \frac{\text{Change in S}}{\text{Change in Y}} \qquad APS = \frac{S}{Y}$$

(ii) **The distribution of income** High-income consumers save more than low-income consumers. MPS and APS both increase as Y increases. A redistribution of income from low-income to high-income consumers will increase S.

(iii) **Interest rates** High interest rates will encourage individuals to save.

(iv) **Availability of financial institutions** The more banks, building societies, etc., which exist, the more opportunity individuals have to save.

(v) **Government policy** Government fiscal policy will affect S. If the government operates progressive taxes and welfare payments to low-income individuals, S will decline. This is because low-income earners have a low MPS.

(f) INVESTMENT (I)

Investment (I) is an injection into Y, and any increase in I will increase Y. Investment is spending on the creation of capital goods such as factories, buildings, machinery. These capital goods can create more capital goods or consumer goods. Gross investment includes the creation of all new capital goods. However, some of this investment is to replace worn-out existing capital goods (a process termed depreciation). Therefore net investment is gross investment minus depreciation.

Determinants of I

(i) **Expected yields from the investment** This is itself determined by business expectations for the future and existing economic indicators like the level of unemployment, inflation and economic growth.

(ii) **The cost of the investment** This is determined by the rate of interest prevailing in the economy. The money for the investment will mean a forgone rate of interest.

(iii) **New techniques and inventions** New technology may encourage new industries and firms to develop.

(iv) **Government policy** Government itself can stimulate investment by building new roads, schools, hospitals, etc. This may set off a *multiplier effect* which will create even more investment, jobs and incomes. If government builds a new motorway, this creates jobs and incomes directly for people involved in its construction. These people then spend their incomes on a wide range of of consumer goods, creating jobs and incomes in other industries. These people then demand consumer goods. The process continues, eventually creating many more jobs and incomes than those resulting directly from the initial motorway development.

MC1 Which of the following would be regarded by an economist to be investment?
(*a*)   buying gilt-edged securities
(*b*)   building a new factory
(*c*)   depositing money in a building society
(*d*)   buying ordinary shares
(*e*)   opening an investment account with the National Savings Bank

MC2 Which of the following would reduce the level of national income?
(*a*)   an increase in savings
(*b*)   an increase in consumer spending
(*c*)   an increase in exports
(*d*)   a reduction in taxation
(*e*)   a reduction in imports

MC3 Which of the following will *not* increase consumer spending?
(*a*)   an increase in disposable income
(*b*)   a decrease in income tax
(*c*)   an increase in the hire purchase repayment period
(*d*)   a decrease in value added tax
(*e*)   an increase in interest rates

MC4   Which of the following is an injection into the circular flow of income?
(a)   savings
(b)   taxation
(c)   exports
(d)   consumption
(e)   imports

MC5   The marginal propensity to consume is
(a)   the total amount spent on consumption
(b)   the proportion of total income spent on consumption
(c)   the amount people wish to spend on consumption
(d)   consumption during a given period of time
(e)   the proportion of additional income which is spent on consumption

2   THE MEASUREMENT OF NATIONAL INCOME

(a) OUTPUT, EXPENDITURE AND INCOME

The national income is the money value of all goods and services produced in an economy over a given period of time. The statistics relating to the national income are presented every year in an official publication known as the 'Blue Book' of national income statistic.

There are three methods of calculating national income, and they all equal each other. These are: the output method, the expenditure method and the income method.

(i) THE OUTPUT METHOD

The output method adds together the value of all goods and services produced in a country in a year. This gives Total Domestic Product.

		Total Domestic Product
less		stock appreciation
add		residual error
	→	Gross Domestic Product at factor cost
add		net property income from abroad
	→	Gross National Product at factor cost
less		capital consumption (depreciation)
	→	national income

(ii) THE EXPENDITURE METHOD

The expenditure method adds together all money spent by private citizens, firms and the government within the year. This includes consumer spending and investment. This gives Total Domestic Expenditure.

		Total Domestic Expenditure
add		exports
less		imports
	→	Gross Domestic Product at market prices
less		taxes
add		subsidies
	→	Gross Domestic Product at factor cost
add		net property income from abroad
	→	Gross National Product at factor cost
less		capital consumption (depreciation)
	→	national income

(iii) THE INCOME METHOD

The income method adds together all the incomes earned by a country's citizens in a year. It includes wages, rent, interest and profits. The latter includes profits of companies and the surpluses of public corporation. This gives Total Domestic Income.

		Total Domestic Income
less		stock appreciation
plus		residual error
	→	Gross Domestic Product at factor cost
add		net property income from abroad
	→	Gross National Product at factor cost
less		capital consumption (depreciation)
	→	national income

To understand these three methods you need to know the meaning of some of the terms used in the calculations:

Stock appreciation . . . the value of stocks may have risen due to inflation, and this has no connection with output. This must be excluded from the statistics.

Residual error . . . an allowance for errors made in the calculations. It ensures that equality exists between the three methods.

Net property income from abroad . . . the net amount of flows of interest, profits and dividends flowing to UK citizens from abroad and to foreigners from the UK. A plus item represents a net inflow into the UK.

Capital consumption (depreciation) . . . some of the country's output is needed to replace buildings, plant, equipment and vehicles which have become worn out.

Gross Domestic Product (GDP) . . . the total value of goods and services produced in one country.

GDP at factor cost GDP less taxes and plus subsidies. It is what the producer actually receives.

Gross National Product (GNP) . . . GDP plus net property income from abroad.

GNP at factor cost . . . GDP at factor cost plus net property income from abroad.

(b) DIFFICULTIES IN MEASURING THE NATIONAL INCOME

(i) INCOMPLETE INFORMATION

Much work is done by individuals for themselves, which is not included in the statistics. There is also much work done in the 'black economy' for which no records are kept, and this also is not included.

(ii) IMPUTED VALUES

Some self-supplied goods and services are given an imputed value – for instance, owner-occupied houses and the value of food consumed by farmers themselves.

(iii) TRANSFER PAYMENTS

Income from state welfare schemes which does not represent payment for a good or service provided. These are excluded from the statistics.

(iv) DOUBLE COUNTING

There is a danger that some output may be counted twice. We must exclude the value of inputs if they have already been counted.

(v) THE SERVICES OF HOUSEWIVES

Similar work may not be included in the statistics. For instance, housework done by housewives is not included but the same work done by a paid employee is.

(vi) INFLATION

Inflation distorts statistics from year to year. The same national output may appear larger if inflation has occurred during the time period.

(vii) DEPRECIATION

The value given to depreciation is an arbitrary figure.

(c) **THE USES OF NATIONAL INCOME STATISTICS**

National income statistics have four main uses:
(i)   As an instrument of economic planning and review.
(ii)   As a means of indicating changes in a country's standard of living.
(iii)   As a means of comparing the economic performance of different countries.
(iv)   To indicate changes in the economic growth of a country.

(i)   AS AN INSTRUMENT OF ECONOMIC PLANNING AND REVIEW

The statistics provide important background information on which the government can base its decisions. Private enterprise firms can also use the statistics to assess future prospects. The figures help in answering numerous questions, such as whether the economy is growing and at what rate. Which industries are declining and which expanding? What is happening to consumer spending, savings and investment?

(ii) AS A MEANS OF INDICATING CHANGES IN A COUNTRY'S STANDARD OF LIVING

National income statistics are used to assess changes in the standard of living within a country. If the national income increases, it is normally assumed that the standard of living has improved. However, this may not be the case and certain factors have to be taken into account:
–   National income statistics may be expressed in market (or current) prices and therefore show an increase due to inflation. Much better is real national income or national income at constant prices, where statistics are expressed as an index of prices.
–   To calculate national income at constant prices for Year 10:

$$\text{national income at market prices} \times \frac{100 \text{ (base year price index)}}{\text{price index of Year 10}}$$

–   National income must be related to the size of population. When national income is divided by the total population, this gives national income per head (or per capita). Another problem, however, is that this says nothing about the distribution of income.
–   The increase in national income may be accompanied by high social costs such as pollution, congestion and damage to the environment. There may be less leisure time.
–   The national income increase may be due to more exports (and fewer goods for home consumption) or more defence spending. Both these situations may not improve citizens' standard of living.
–   National income statistics say nothing about the quality of output.

(iii)   AS A MEANS OF COMPARING THE ECONOMIC PERFORMANCE OF DIFFERENT COUNTRIES

National income statistics give a guide to the standard of living in two different countries. Again there are difficulties.

–   The statistics may be calculated differently.

–   To avoid the effects of inflation and population size, the statistics are best presented as real national income per capita.

–   What about the distribution of income?

–   There is the problem of the exchange rate between the currencies of the two countries.

–   The size of unrecorded transactions may differ between the two countries.

–   The two countries may have different cultures and climates, therefore commodities required in one country are not in demand in the other.

–   National income statistics tell us nothing about the number of doctors per head of population, the availability of leisure activities, the crime rate or the number of people physically or mentally ill.

(iv)   TO INDICATE CHANGES IN ECONOMIC GROWTH OF A COUNTRY

The best indicator of economic growth is changes in real national income per captia. However, frequently growth is expressed in terms of percentage changes in GNP.

Economic growth is usually thought to be desirable because it means a better standard of living for citizens and more wealth to be allocated. More money can be spent on education, health and defence.

Nevertheless, economic growth may involve social costs, as indicated on p.154. Indeed, economic growth does not necessarily bring happiness and total well-being.

It is a fact that the UK's recent economic growth in the 1960s and 1970s has been somewhat disappointing compared to that of other advanced industrial countries such as Japan, West Germany and France. The reasons for this may include:

–   poor management;

–   damage done by industrial disputes;

–   education not fitting industry's needs and requirements;

–   lack of investment in new technology;

–   propping up old and declining industry;

–   government taxation policy reducing the amount of money industry has for investment;

–   constant changes in government economic policy – high interest rates, high exchanges rates, reflation followed by deflation.

–   low quality and quantity of labour;

–   low levels of productivity (see p.123).

MC6 In calculating national income, which of the following should be included?
(*a*)   food consumed and grown by farmers themselves
(*b*)   old age pensions
(*c*)   unemployment benefits
(*d*)   money given by a man to his wife, to cover housekeeping expenses
(*e*)   student grants

MC7

	£000m
Total domestic spending at market prices	40
Exports and property income from abroad	10
Imports and property income paid abroad	16
Taxes on spending	6
Subsidies	2

From the above figures, the Gross National Product at factor cost is:
(*a*)   £30,000m
(*b*)   £34,000m
(*c*)   £38,000m
(*d*)   £42,000m
(*e*)   £46,000m

MC8 Which of the following is *not* included in the calculation of Gross National Product at factor cost?
(*a*)   dividends paid to British investors abroad
(*b*)   undistributed profits made by private enterprise companies
(*c*)   fares received by British Rail
(*d*)   excise duty on tobacco
(*e*)   wages paid to a teacher

MC9 Which of the following is most likely to be found in a country with a high standard of living?
(*a*)   a low life expectancy
(*b*)   a low level of economic growth
(*c*)   a high per capita income
(*d*) ·   a high level of inflation
(*e*)   a high infant mortality rate

MC10 Measures of changes in economic growth can best seen by changes in the
(*a*)   level of unemployment
(*b*)   balance of payments statistics
(*c*)   terms of trade index
(*d*)   per capita national income
(*e*)   Retail Price Index

EXTENDED WRITING QUESTIONS

1 (*a*) Distinguish between (i) Gross Domestic Product (GDP), (ii) Gross National Product (GNP), and (iii) national income.
(*b*) Outline the main problems in calculating national income statistics.
(*c*) Explain why a rise in the national income of a country does not necessarily mean a rise in the standard of living.

2 (*a*) Briefly explain the three methods of measuring national income.
(*b*) For what purposes might national income statistics be used?
(*c*) How can the level of national income be increased?
(*d*) Give two possible advantages and two disadvantages for an economy of an increasing national income.

3 (*a*) Distinguish between the terms (i) capital goods and (ii) consumer goods as used by an economist. Give one example of each kind of good.
(*b*) Examine the possible effects of the introduction of more capital formation on an economy.
(*c*) What difficulties do developing countries face in acquiring capital goods?

4 (*a*) What is meant by 'the circular flow of income'?
(*b*) (i) Distinguish between injections into and the withdrawals from the circular flow.
(ii) Give three injections and three withdrawals.
(*c*) How might an increase in any one injection affect the circular flow of income?

5 (*a*) What is meant by 'economic growth'?
(*b*) Outline the main factors which may increase the rate of economic growth in an economy.
(*c*) Discuss the possible relationships between increasing economic growth and consumer welfare.

DATA RESPONSE

The table below relates to the national income of Country A and the Retail Price Index.

	Money national Income	Retail Price Index
Year 1	£10,000	100
Year 2	£11,000	105
Year 3	£12,000	110
Year 4	£13,000	120

(*a*) Distinguish between (i) the cost of living and (ii) the standard of living.
(*b*) How are (i) the cost of living and (ii) the standard of living measured?

(c)   What is the difference between real national income and money national income?

(d)   Calculate the change (if any) in real national income of Country A

        (i) between years 1 and 2

        (ii) between years 3 and 4.

(e)   In Year 4 Country B has a money national income of £15,000. Does this means that Country B has a better standard of living than Country A? Explain your answer.

Answer

(a)   The cost of living is a measure of the price of goods and services in general throughout the economy. If prices in general are increasing, the cost of living has increased.

    The standard of living is a measure of the availability of goods and services to consumers in the country. An increasing standard of living means that more goods and services are available to consumers. This implies increasing real incomes.

(b)   The cost of living is measured by measuring the rate of inflation. This is achieved by the Retail Price Index, which is dealt with on pp.156–7. The standard of living is measured by the indicator real national income per head. An increase in real national income per head indicates a rising standard of living. Real national income per head takes into account both rising population and rising inflation, so it indicates a real increase in standard of living per head of population (one difficulty is that it says nothing about distribution of income between people in the country!).

(c)   Money national income is the measure of national income at present-day prices (current market prices). Real national income takes into account rising prices. In a period of inflation money national income will inevitably rise, because prices are generally rising. This does not indicate that more goods and services are really available. A rise in real national income does indicate a better standard of living because the national income is measured in prices constant to one year (known as the base year) and compared to all other years whose prices are similarly expressed in the prices of the base year.

(d)   To calculate real national income for Year 1, use the formula:

$$\text{Money national income for Year 1} \times \frac{100 \ (\text{Index number of base year})}{\text{Retail Price Index number of Year 1}}$$

Let us apply this to the question.

        (i) *Between Year 1 and Year 2*

$$£11,000 \times \frac{100}{105} = £10,476$$

So between Year 1 and Year 2 real national income did increase from £10,000 to £10,476.

(ii) *Between Year 3 and Year 4*

Real national income of Year 3 . . . $£12,000 \times \dfrac{100}{110} = £10,909$

Real national income of Year 4 . . . $£13,000 \times \dfrac{100}{120} = £10,833$

Between Year 3 and Year 4 real national income fell from £10,909 to £10,833.

(e)   There are several difficulties in using money national income statistics to indicate differences between the standards of living in different countries. These problems are well documented on p.155.

Answers to multiple-choice questions:

MC1	(b)		MC6	(a)
MC2	(a)		MC7	(a)
MC3	(e)		MC8	(d)
MC4	(c)		MC9	(c)
MC5	(e)		MC10	(d)

INFLATION AND UNEMPLOYMENT

CONTENTS

A study of inflation and unemployment is essential in our study of economics. This chapter is subdivided as follows:

1 INFLATION
The meaning of inflation.
The Retail Price Index.
The problems of inflation.
The causes of inflation: demand pull, monetary theory, cost push.
Anti-inflation policies.

2 UNEMPLOYMENT
The meaning of unemployment.
The problems of unemployment.
Types of unemployment.
Causes of worsening unemployment in the UK since the early 1970s.
Policies to reduce unemployment . . . demand side and supply side measures.

The two main priorities of any government will be to reduce the levels of unemployment and inflation. The main difficulty appears to be achieving the two objectives together.

1 INFLATION

(a) THE MEANING OF INFLATION

Inflation is a general and persistent rise in the prices of goods and services. It is indicated by percentage changes in the *Retail Price Index* and varies from year to year. In the UK inflation for much of the post-1945 period was around 3 per cent. In the 1970s inflation began to increase and in 1975 reached 24 per cent. Since 1980 inflation has varied between 3 per cent and 10 per cent p.a. In 1987 inflation was 4 per cent.

When inflation reaches very high percentages it is termed *hyper-inflation*, as experienced in some South American countries, where prices rise by over 100 per cent p.a. The opposite to inflation is *deflation*, which is falling prices. *Disinflation* is a slowing down in the inflation rate and *reflation* is the increasing of demands in the economy which have inflationary effects. '*Slumpflation*' or '*stagflation*' is high levels of inflation coexisting with high levels of unemployment.

(b) THE RETAIL PRICE INDEX

Changes in the cost of living are measured by changes in prices.

Inflation is measured by changes in the Retail Price Index (RPI), which measures changes in the average price of a collection of goods and services contained in an average family's spending. The data are collected by the Department of Employment. A long list of items is included, divided into eleven broad groups (e.g. food, alcoholic drink, housing, clothing and footwear, etc.

The goods and services are 'weighted' to indicate their importance in terms of the weekly expenditure spent on each item. A base year is given an index number value of 100 (the most recent base year is 1987) and all prices are compared to the base year. If prices of commodities in the Index rose by 10 per cent by 'base year plus 1', the new Index would be 101.

The Retail Price Index has its problems:
  –   What is the meaning of 'average basket of goods and services' and the 'average family'?
  –   The weights have to be changed frequently to indicate changes in spending patterns.
  –   A single figure does not indicate differences in price changes between commodities.
  –   The RPI says nothing about changes in quality and performance of commodities.

The RPI is of more than just academic interest. It forms the basis of many wage negotiations, up-rating social security benefits and pensions and affects measurement of the real level of national income and government spending.

You should be able to perform simple tasks to show your understanding of index number data. Look at this example.

An unweighted Index

Year 1 (base year)			Year 2		
Commodity	Price	Index	Commodity	Price	Index
A	5p	100	A	10p	200
B	20p	100	B	30p	150
C	£1.50	100	C	£2.00	133.3
		300			483.3

Price Index Year 1 = $3\overline{)300}$
                  = 100

Price Index Year 2 = $3\overline{)483.3}$
                  = 161.1

Prices rose from 100 in year 1 to 161.1 in Year 2, which is a 61.1% increase.

A weighted Index

Year 1 (base year)

Commodity	Price	Weight	Index	Weighted Index
A	5p	1	100	100
B	20p	3	100	300
C	£1.50p	6	100	600
		10		1000

Price Index = 10 ⌐1000   (weighted Index ÷ sum of weights)
        = 100

Year 2

Commodity	Price	Weight	Index	Weighted Index
A	10p	1	200	200
B	30p	3	150	450
C	£2.00p	6	133.3	799.8
		10		1449.8

Price Index = 10 ⌐1449.8   (weighted Index ÷ sum of weights)
        = 144.9

Therefore the average price movement according to the weighted Index is from 100 in Year 1 (base year) to 144.9 in Year 2. Prices have increased by 44.9%.

(c) THE PROBLEMS OF INFLATION

Inflation is regarded as undesirable for the following reasons:

(i) INFLATION CAUSES SOCIAL INJUSTICE

People on relatively fixed incomes (perhaps depending on government for grants and benefits) find that increases in their income rarely keep pace with inflation. This means that their real incomes (money income in terms of the goods and services it can buy) will diminish. This may apply to students, pensioners and the unemployed.

(ii) INFLATION MAY WORSEN THE BALANCE OF PAYMENTS

Inflation will result in the prices of UK exports rising and the relative prices of imports falling. Given elastic demand (see p.33), the value of exports will fall and the value of imports will rise. Foreign producers will begin to dominate the home market and UK jobs and incomes will be lost.

(iii) INFLATION RESULTS IN CREDITORS (LENDERS) LOSING MONEY

Lenders will lose money because what they receive back will be worth less. This will discourage savings, which partly determine the level of investment. Less investment results in fewer jobs and incomes.

(iv) INFLATION DISCOURAGES BUSINESS CONFIDENCE

Businessmen become concerned about the level of inflation and may decide not to invest.

(v) INFLATION MAY DEVELOP INTO HYPERINFLATION

Inflation may worsen and lead to a complete lack of confidence in the value of money. The economy will begin to break down and this may allow extreme political groups to seize power. Economists point to the rise of Hitler during the hyperinflation period of the late 1920s and early 1930s in Germany.

Despite these problems with inflation, some economists argue that a *low* level of inflation can be desirable. For instance, it may indicate high demand and stimulate business confidence and investment. The government may benefit from more tax revenue because people's incomes rise and they pay more taxes. The government may also benefit from a drop in the value of interest repayments to holders of government securities.

On the whole, however, inflation is regarded as bad and governments aim to reduce its level.

(d) THE CAUSES OF INFLATION

The causes of inflation are the subject of discussion and disagreement amongst economists and politicians. We need to know what causes inflation to determine the appropriate remedies. Three main theories are put forward:

(i) THE DEMAND-PULL THEORY OF INFLATION

If there is too much demand in the economy relative to the supply of goods and services, prices will rise. The excessive demand may be due to:

– too much government spending . . . large budget deficits (see p.188) will result in too much demand in the economy;

– too much consumer spending . . . perhaps due to excessive incomes and easy bank credit. Consumers have more money in their pockets and demand increases.

Demand-pull inflation is usually associated with low unemployment, because the excessive demand leads to an increase in production. There is, however, a variety of demand-pull inflation which suggests that inflation can exist despite high levels of unemployment. This is the monetarist theory of inflation.

(ii) THE MONETARIST THEORY OF INFLATION

Monetarists argue that too much money in the economy causes inflation. An economist named Milton Friedman has said, 'Inflation is always a purely monetary phenomenon.' The argument goes that too much money circulating in the economy leads to prices increasing. The basis of the argument is the *quantity theory of money*, which states that

$$MV = PT$$

where

M is the money supply
V is the velocity of circulation of money (the number of times money changes hands)
P is the price level
T is the value of output.

Monetarists state that in the short term V and T remain stable. Consequently, an increase in M causes an increase in P. Thus inflation exists without an increase in production and employment.

(iii) THE COST-PUSH THEORY OF INFLATION

Some economists argue that prices are pushed up by increases in the costs of production. This may be due to an increase in raw material prices or an increase in incomes to the labour force not matched by an increase in output. The costs per unit rise and so will prices to consumers. Cost-pushers argue that the slumpflation of the early 1970s onwards was a cost-push inflation caused by the fourfold increase in world oil prices in 1973–74.

(e) ANTI-INFLATION POLICIES

The remedies employed by any government to combat inflation are determined by what it perceives to be in the main cause of the problem.

(i) REMEDIES FOR DEMAND-PULL INFLATION

The main aim of policies to reduce demand-pull inflation would be to diminish the aggregate level of demand in the economy. This could be achieved by the following measures:

Reducing the government's fiscal budget deficit (see p.188). Higher taxes and/or lower government spending will reduce demand in the economy.

Reducing consumer demand by tighter hire purchase restrictions. This may involve higher interest rates, shorter repayment periods and a larger initial deposit. Consumer bank credit could be made less available by increasing interest rates and by Bank of England directives to the commercial banks (see p.211).

Tighter control over money supply ... This would be the main remedy according to the monetarist view of inflation.

(ii) REMEDIES FOR THE MONETARIST VIEW OF INFLATION

The monetarists believe that there is only one cause of inflation: too much money. Therefore policies aimed at reducing the level of money in the economy should be followed. This would involve tight controls over bank credit through higher interest rates, directives, special deposits and open-market operations. These measures are all discussed on pp.210–11.

The government itself should also print less money and cut down its borrowing.

Monetarists have several monetary targets which should be carefully observed. These are:

> Mo = Notes and coins in circulation plus bank holdings of cash in tills plus bank deposits held at the Bank of England.
>
> MI = notes and coins in circulation plus money in bank current accounts.
>
> Sterling M3 = MI plus money in bank deposit accounts.
>
> M3 = Sterling M3 plus holdings of foreign currencies by UK citizens and firms.

Monetarists judge the success of their policies by how much (or how little) these monetary targets rise in a given period.

The Thatcher Conservative government 1979– has pursued monetarist remedies for inflation. This government has been criticized by opponents for following too rigorous a monetarist approach. Controls on money supply, tight fiscal measures and high interest rates have worsened unemployment and inhibited economic growth. Some critics suggest that 'the cure is worse than the disease'. However, the government does argue that inflation has been reduced to below 5 per cent p.a. in 1986 and 1987.

(iii) REMEDIES FOR COST-PUSH INFLATION

'Cost-pushers' argue that the main remedy for inflation is some kind of *'prices and incomes policy'* to control increases in both prices and incomes. The UK has had several periods when such policies have been introduced. Sometimes they are compulsory, as in 1972–4, and sometimes voluntary and subject to persuasion and coercion, as in 1976–9 (the so-called 'social contract').

Arguments in favour of a prices and incomes policy

It ensures social justice. It means that the powerful groups in society (i.e. firms and trade unions) are not able to gain advantage.

It does not worsen unemployment, as perhaps the monetarist remedy does.

It deals with the main cause of inflation, i.e. high wage costs.

Arguments against a prices and incomes policy

Demand-pullers and monetarists would argue that it is not dealing with the main causes of inflation.

Such a policy involves either agreed flat-rate increases in incomes or agreed percentage increases. Flat-rate increases are unpopular with the higher-paid groups because as a proportion of existing income any increase will be low.

Percentage-rate increases are unpopular with the lower-paid groups because they receive less in income terms (10 per cent of £5,000 is less than 10 per cent of £10,000).

Prices and incomes policies eventually break down as certain groups of workers plead that they are a 'special case' for a wage increase. Workers feel that wages are controlled but not other incomes like rents, profits or interest payments.

MC1 Which one of the following groups is most likely to benefit from inflation?
(a)   exporters
(b)   debtors
(c)   creditors
(d)   pensioners
(e)   entrepeneurs.

MC2 Changes in the value of money are measured by the
(a)   level of productivity
(b)   level of earnings
(c)   level of interest rates
(d)   Terms of Trade Index
(e)   Retail Price Index.

MC3 Which of the following must be a result of inflation?
(a)   higher interest rates (i.e. the cost of borrowing money)
(b)   a rise in the exchange rate
(c)   an increase in the value of money
(d)   a reduction in the value of money
(e)   less money is printed.

MC4 The following are assumed to be initial causes of inflation. Which would be described as 'cost-push'?
(a)   an increase in imported oil prices
(b)   an increase in money supply

(c)   an increase in unemployment benefits

(d)   a reduction in income tax

(e)   a reduction in deposits needed for hire purchase.

MC5 Which of the following is likely to cause demand-pull inflation?

(a)   an increase in imported oil prices

(b)   a reduced budget deficit

(c)   an increased budget deficit

(d)   an increase in wage rates

(e)   a fall in the external value of the pound sterling.

2   UNEMPLOYMENT

A major objective of any government is to achieve full employment (or at least to reduce the level of unemployment). Unemployment has been a major economic problem since the early 1970s, when the numbers of unemployed began to increase dramatically. By 1986/87 about 3¼ million people were registered as unemployed; this is approximately 14 per cent of the working population.

(a) THE MEANING OF UNEMPLOYMENT

There is some controversy about what exactly is meant by unemployment. It was once defined as all those people between the ages of sixteen and sixty-five who were willing and able to work but without a job. However, the official definition is now calculated from the number of people registered as unemployed and in receipt of unemployment benefit. Critics argue that this leads to a lower total of unemployed persons because the following groups may be excluded:

–   people not registering or receiving benefit, like housewives and old people. They may not be eligible for benefits (like many housewives), although they are seeking work.

–   males over the age of sixty.

–   young people over the age of sixteen who are on government training schemes (such as YTS).

–   school leavers who may not have been unemployed long enough to qualify for benefits.

However, some people are included in the statistics who may already have found employment by the time the statistics are published. Also, some of those included regard themselves as retired or may be sick or disabled.

(b) THE PROBLEMS OF UNEMPLOYMENT

Any government is concerned about the level of unemployed, for the following reasons:

–   The financial cost of the taxpayer of financing unemployment benefit.

–   The economic waste of having scarce labour not being fully utilized.

–   The low standard of living of unemployed people and the loss of tax income from taxpayers.

–   Social and health problems may arise within unemployed families.

–   Crime and vandalism may be associated with high levels of unemployment.

–   A government which allows unemployment to rise is viewed with disfavour by the electorate.

(c) TYPES OF UNEMPLOYMENT

(i) Seasonal unemployment Some work is of a seasonal nature, such as work in the construction and tourist industries.

(ii) Frictional unemployment Some workers may be unemployed despite there being vacancies elsewhere in the economy. Such workers are in the process of looking for work.

This type of unemployment is closely associated with geographical and occupational immobility (see p.122). It is sometimes called transitional (or normal) unemployment.

(iii) Cyclical unemployment (also known as mass unemployment). This is unemployment characterized by a lack in aggregate demand throughout the economy and in virtually all industries. It was present during the depression of the 1920s and 1930s and has also prevailed since the early 1970s in the UK.

(iv) Structural unemployment This is unemployment amongst workers in certain industries which are in decline. Traditionally in the UK there have been four main declining industries: coal, steel, textiles and shipbuilding. Since the early 1970s manufacturing industry in general, and motor vehicles in particular, have also suffered structural unemployment. Again it is associated with immobility of labour.

(v) Regional unemployment This is unemployment in the high-unemployment, regionally depressed areas such as Wales, Scotland, North England and Northern Ireland. It is closely associated with structural unemployment.

(vi) Technological unemployment This is unemployment caused by the introduction of labour-saving new technology.

(vii) Voluntary unemployment There may be a percentage of the unemployed who for a variety of reasons may wish to be without work.

(viii) Residual unemployment Some people are deemed to be unemployable because of mental or physical problems.

(d) CAUSES OF WORSENING UNEMPLOYMENT IN THE UK SINCE THE EARLY 1970s

Unemployment has worsened quite dramatically since the early 1970s. Several reasons can be put forward to explain this:

(i) The world recession (slumpflation) since the *rise in oil prices* in 1973–4. The rise in oil prices increased production costs; therefore employers shed labour to keep costs per unit as low as possible. Also, countries had to spend more of their income on oil and had less to spend on manufactured commodities. The UK is regarded as mainly a manufacturing country.

(ii) Government policies to reduce the level of inflation (again mainly caused by rising oil prices) involved deflationary fiscal and monetary policies. These reduced the level of aggregate demand in the economy and worsened unemployment.

(iii) Technological innovations have led to the replacement of people by machines.

(iv) Foreign competition (especially from Japan) has led to a decline in demand for UK commodities at home and abroad. Foreign goods have been cheaper and better than similar UK products in many areas (e.g. the car industry).

(v) High wage costs People in jobs, through their trade unions, have managed to win high wages and employers have been forced to make many people redundant to keep costs per unit as low as possible.

(e) POLICIES TO REDUCE UNEMPLOYMENT

Any government has open to it a number of policy options it can pursue in an attempt to reduce unemployment. A government could operate on the demand side of the economy or on the supply side of the economy.

(i) DEMAND-SIDE MEASURES

These measures attempt to increase the level of aggregate demand and are regarded as reflationary (see p.163):
–   Increase the size of the fiscal budget deficit by increasing governmental spending and/or reducing taxation.
–   Increase public and private investment on the infrastructure in the economy. Public investment programmes will set off a 'multiplier effect' through the economy.
–   Increase consumer spending by loosening restrictions on hire

purchase, lowering interest rates and making credit available. This would involve expansion of the money supply.

– Help the assisted areas by spending more on regional policy.

– Introduce tariffs to protect jobs. However, this would involve problems (see p.242).

The Thatcher Conservative government (1979–) has not adopted demand-side measures because it believes that such measures would cause too much demand in the economy and worsen inflation. Instead, this government has concentrated on measures to stimulate the supply side of the economy.

(ii) SUPPLY-SIDE MEASURES

– Improve education and training so that they are more appropriate to industry's needs (e.g. YTS scheme). The government has overseen the introduction of the Certificate of Pre-Vocational Education (CPVE), the Training and Vocational Education Initiative (TVEI) and even the General Certificate of Secondary Education (GCSE).

– Improve the geographical and occupational mobility of labour (see p.122) by retraining schemes, etc.

– Keep wage costs as low as possible to make workers more employable.

– Adjust the tax system to make it more worthwhile for the unemployed to get work, e.g. reduce the lower rates of basic tax and increase personal allowances to reduce the 'poverty trap' (see p.186).

– Reduce the employer's contribution to National Insurance.

– Encourage new small firms, especially in the new technologies.

– Encourage work-sharing schemes whereby jobs are spread around more part-time workers.

– Improve labour-market information about jobs and vacancies, etc.

– Raise the school-leaving age and reduce the retirement age. This is unlikely in the near future because of the cost to the taxpayer.

MC6 Which one of the following regions has the lowest rate of unemployment?
(a)   South Wales
(b)   West Midlands
(c)   South-East England
(d)   Northern Ireland
(e)   Scotland

For questions **MC7** and **MC8** select from the list (a) to (e) the unemployment term that is described:
(a)   frictional unemployment
(b)   structural unemployment
(c)   seasonal unemployment

(d)   technological unemployment
(e)   mass unemployment

MC7 A steel worker is unemployed because of the fall in demand for British Steel.

MC8 The government increases taxes and reduces public spending, which reduces the level of demand in the economy and increases unemployment throughout the UK economy.

MC9 In order to try to reduce the level of unemployment the government may
(a)   budget for a deficit
(b)   increase interest rates
(c)   increase taxes
(d)   reduce money supply
(e)   reduce government spending

MC10 Which of the following would be most likely *not* to increase the level of unemployment?
(a)   an increase in indirect taxes
(b)   an increase in interest rates
(c)   a decrease in spending on regional aid
(d)   a decrease in direct taxes
(e)   a decrease in consumer spending

EXTENDED WRITING QUESTIONS

1 (a)   Describe four types of unemployment which may exist in an economy at any one time.
(b)   Examine the causes of the increase in unemployment in the UK since 1970.
(c)   Discuss the methods that can be used to reduce the level of unemployment in the UK.

Answer
To answer part (a) you can describe any four of the following types of unemployment: seasonal, frictional, cyclical, structural (regional), technological, residual and voluntary. All these types are dealt with on p.171.

To answer (b) you need to discuss the recession in Western economies sincce the early 1970s. Relate this to high oil prices during this period and the so-called 'sumpflation' (or 'stagflation'). Other factors which need to be discussed as factors contributing to unemployment are government deflationary monetary and fiscal policies adopted to overcome inflation. Technological improvements, foreign competitors and high wage costs have all made a contribution.

To answer (c) you need to differentiate between 'demand-side' and 'supply-side' policies which may be adopted. Demand-side measures might include higher government spending (relate to the multiplier concept), lower taxes, reflationary monetary and fiscal measures and even protectionist measures to deter imports. Supply-side measures might include policies to improve geographical and occupational mobility of labour, YTS schemes, reduce income tax to motivate hard work, encourage small firms and improve labour-market information.

2   (*a*)   What is meant by immobility of labour?
     (*b*)   What are the main causes of immobility of labour?
     (*c*)   (i) Why is it desirable to encourage mobility of labour?
         (ii) How can mobility of labour be achieved?

3   (*a*)   Define the term 'inflation'.
     (*b*)   Outline the main causes of inflation.
     (*c*)   Which groups may (i) benefit and (ii) suffer during a period of inflation?
     (*d*)   Discuss the methods that might be used to reduce the level of inflation in the economy.

4   (*a*)   Distinguish between (i) cost-push and (ii) demand-pull inflation.
     (*b*)   Describe the main features of an incomes policy.
     (*c*)   What problems may be encountered by a government when trying to implement such a policy?
     (*d*)   What are the alternatives to incomes policy as a remedy for inflation?

5   (*a*)   What is meant by the phrase 'the supply of money'?
     (*b*)   'Monetarists believe that inflation is always and everywhere a monetary phenomenon.' What is the meaning of this statement?
     (*c*)   How can the government control the growth of money supply?
     (*d*)   Why does the government wish to reduce the level of inflation?

DATA RESPONSE

UK unemployment and unfilled vacancies

(*a*)   How do government statisticians define unemployment? (Make reference to those groups who are included and excluded from these unemployment statistics.)

(*b*)   Why do you think unemployment increased from 2,980,000 in January 1983 to 3,110,000 in December 1984?

(*c*)   (i) Discuss the relationship between the total number of unemployed and the number of unfilled vacancies.
         (ii) How do you account for this relationship?
         (iii) Give one consequence for the unemployed if this relationship continues.

(*d*)   Why do some regions in the country suffer levels of unemployment higher than the average for the UK?

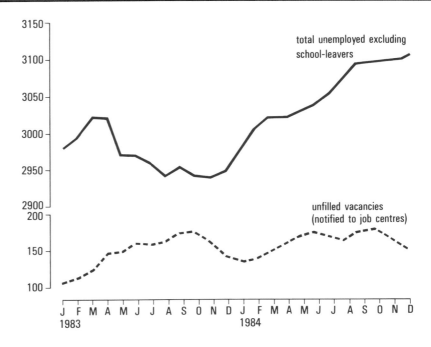

Source: *Monthly Digest of Statistics*, January 1985

(*e*)   What measures can the government take to reduce the level of unemployment within the UK?

Inflation at 3pc and 'still falling'

INFLATION was down to 3 per cent last month — its lowest level for 18 years.

The fall is mainly due to cheaper home loans and petrol price cuts.

Water rates, cigarettes, second-hand cars, bus fares, electricity went up with local council rates and rents but bacon, margarine and fresh vegetable prices came down.

Employment Minister Kenneth Clarke said: 'This is unqualified good news for our general economic prospects.'

Source: *Daily Mail*

PRICE CHANGES SINCE THE SWINGING SIXTIES

Item	1968 price	Today	Difference
Av. wage	£20	£192	+860%
Income Tax	41p/£	29p	−29.3%
Av. Semi	£4,500	£34,800	+673%
Ford Escort	£927	£4,921	+430%
Loaf	16p	48p	+200%
Beer	6p/pint	90p	+1,400%
Whisky	£2.42	£8.20	+238%
Cigarettes (20)	29p	£1.50	+417%
Petrol	30p/gallon	£1.60	+433%
Stamp	2p	17p	+750%
Daily Paper	2p	20p	+900%
Haircut	25p	£4	+1,500%
Fridge	£60	£150	+150%
TV	£90	£250	+180%

(a)   With reference to the statement 'Inflation was down to 3 per cent last month', explain
  (i) the meaning of inflation
  (ii) how inflation is measured.
(b)   How do you account for varying price changes in this period between different goods and services?
(c)   (i) What is the difference between money wages and real wages?
  (ii) What has happened to money wages and real wages during the period analysed by the price changes here?
(d)   How do you account for the decline in inflation from just below 20 per cent in 1980 to 3 per cent in 1986?

(e)   Why is a low rate of inflation regarded as 'unqualified good news for UK's general economic prospects'?

Answers to multiple-choice questions:

MC1	(b)	MC6	(c)
MC2	(e)	MC7	(b)
MC3	(d)	MC8	(e)
MC4	(a)	MC9	(a)
MC5	(c)	MC10	(d)

PUBLIC FINANCE AND FISCAL POLICY

CONTENTS

Fiscal policy applies to government spending and revenues (taxation) and government borrowing. This chapter is subdivided into the following topics:

1   **Objectives of fiscal policy.**

2   **Government expenditure:**
    Major items of government spending.
    Major sources of revenue.
    Effects of government spending.
    Government spending: good or bad?

3   **Government revenue:**

    Taxation The principles of taxation; progressive, proportional and regressive taxes; direct taxes; indirect taxes; different types of direct and indirect taxes; the effects of taxation.

    Public Sector Borrowing Requirement (PSBR) Budget deficits, budget surpluses and balanced budgets.

4   **Recent fiscal policy and criticisms of this policy.**

1   OBJECTIVES OF FISCAL POLICY

Public finance has a number of important economic, social and political aims and objectives:

(i) To manage the total level of demand in the economy. The government can influence, through its government spending, taxation and borrowing programmes, the level of aggregate (total) demand in the economy, and thereby influence the level of employment, inflation, the nation's trade and economic growth.

(ii) To provide for defence.

(iii) To provide for the forces of law and order and to protect citizens from crime and disorder.

(iv) To improve economic and industrial performance by helping British industry become more efficient and competitive.

(v) To redistribute income so as to help the less well off in society.

2 GOVERNMENT EXPENDITURE

Government (or public) spending is an important aspect of fiscal policy and its aims have already been documented. Government spending includes money spent by central government, by government departments, nationalized industries (see p.97) and local authorities (see pp.111–13). It is the money spent by the government for the benefit of the community in general.

(a) THE MAJOR ITEMS OF GOVERNMENT SPENDING

- Social security
- Education
- Health and social services
- Defence
- National debt interest repayments
- Housing and environment
- Industry and trade
- Roads and transport.

The Thatcher Conservative government (1979–   ) has attempted to restrain government spending within defined limits because it believes that high levels of government expenditure cause excessive demand and thereby are a direct cause of inflation. Inflation has been identified as the main economic evil, which it is a priority to overcome. See Chapter 9 on Inflation.

(b) THE MAJOR SOURCES OF REVENUE
(see pp.183–9 on government revenue)

- Indirect taxes
- Direct taxes
- National Insurance contributions
- Government borrowing
- Rent and interest and receipts from charges for government services.

For up-to-date statistics on government expenditure and revenue, refer to data response question 2 on page 195.

(c) THE EFFECTS OF GOVERNMENT SPENDING

The impact of government spending is determined by the economic, social and political objectives of the government of the day.

(i) It provides for a redistribution of income and wealth. Money is taken from the rich (progressive direct taxation – see p.184) and spent on the less well off in the form of social security, health and social services.

(ii) It provides for improving the quality and quantity of medical services, schools, roads, libraries and museums, etc.

(iii) It provides for more jobs by building roads, hospitals, etc.

(iv) It provides for economic growth by spending money to improve the industrial structure of the economy and the education and health of the British people.

(v) It has effects on the total level of demand in the economy and therefore on prices, jobs and economic growth.

(d) GOVERNMENT SPENDING: GOOD OR BAD?

Opponents of too much government spending argue that it may cause inflation by stimulating too much aggregate demand in the economy. It blunts hard work and incentives because people are over-protected by government handouts, and because high-income earners have to pay proportionately more tax.

Some economists and politicians argue that high levels of government spending in industry are bad because they 'crowd out' private business investment. It is argued that high levels of government spending can be financed by only two main sources: taxation and borrowing. The former is paid partly by businesses, leaving them with less money to invest. The latter will lead to high interest rates.

However, supporters of government spending argue that it should provide for a level of demand in the economy which creates jobs and stimulates economic growth. There will be what is called a 'multiplier effect' in the economy. Government spending on the economic infrastructure (i.e. roads, sewers, schools, hospitals, etc.) will give people jobs and incomes. These people, now employed, spend their incomes, creating jobs in other industries to produce the commodities required. The process continues. It can be used to increase the standard of living and quality of life of the community in general. The British people are better fed, better educated and healthier partly due to high government spending, and in consequence are better able to contribute to economic growth.

MC1 Which of the following categories represents the highest proportion of government spending?
(a)   regional aid
(b)   nationalized industries
(c)   social services
(d)   education
(e)   defence.

---

3 GOVERNMENT REVENUE

There are two main sources of central government revenue, which is used to finance government spending:

(a)   taxation
(b)   borrowing.

Let us look at taxation; we shall discuss borrowing on pp.188–9.

We are discussing here central government revenues and not local government revenues. The latter are dealt with on pp.111–13 and include rates.

(a) TAXATION

(i) THE PRINCIPLES OF TAXATION

In establishing a tax system a government can be guided by four clear principles, often called the canons of taxation, developed by the classical economist Adam Smith.

Certainty The tax should be clearly understood by the payer and the collector. The taxpayer should know how the tax works, how much he has to pay and when it should be paid.

Convenience The tax should be conveniently paid and collected.

Economy The cost of the tax should not exceed the tax receipts.

Equity The tax must be fair – people in exactly the same situation should pay the same amount of tax. Moreover, the tax should be linked with the person's ability to pay.

There are other qualities which a good tax should possess – it should not be a disincentive to effort and work, it should be easy to adjust and should contribute to the government's overall economic policy aims (i.e. to reduce inflation, create jobs, stimulate economic growth, encourage investment, etc.).

(ii) PROGRESSIVE, PROPORTIONAL AND REGRESSIVE TAXES

A progressive tax is one in which the richer citizens pay a proportionately higher percentage of their income as tax.

A proportional tax is one in which all citizens pay the same proportion, in percentage terms, of their income. This means, of course, that a rich taxpayer pays, in total terms, more tax than his/her less-well-off counterpart.

A regressive tax is one in which the less-well-off citizens pay a proportionately higher percentage of their income tax.

All taxes today fall into one of two categories of tax – direct taxes and indirect taxes.

(iii) DIRECT TAXES

Direct taxes fall directly on the taxpayer's income and/or wealth. These taxes are collected, in the UK, by the *Inland Revenue* and include income tax, corporation tax, inheritance tax (formerly capital transfer tax) and capital gains tax. All these taxes are discussed individually on page 186.

Advantages of direct taxes

They are progressive. They therefore help to achieve the social objective of taxing the rich to help the poor in the form of social security payments, etc.

The incidence of the tax (i.e. the person who finally pays the tax) is easily identified. The tax is difficult to shift on to someone else.

The tax does not directly increase prices of commodities.

The tax is cheap and easy to collect, e.g. PAYE for income tax. Indeed, direct taxes conform to the four principles of taxation.

The tax can be used to help achieve government economic objectives. For instance, if the government wishes to create more jobs and economic growth it may reduce direct taxes and thereby increase the level of demand in the economy.

Disadvantages of direct taxes

The taxes may lead to a disincentive to individuals to work hard. Some workers may emigrate abroad and there may be a 'poverty trap' (see p.186).

The taxes may lead to less savings and investment by individuals and firms because they have less income left after tax has been paid.

The taxes encourage tax evasion as people employ accountants to find possible loopholes in the tax system.

The taxpayer has no element of choice in paying the taxes. He/she is clearly identified and has to pay.

(iv) INDIRECT TAXES

Indirect taxes are levied on an individual's (or firm's) expenditures. These taxes are collected, in the UK, by the *Customs and Excise Department*. They include customs duties (see p.240), excise duties (such as tobacco tax, wine and spirits duties and petrol tax) and Value Added Tax (VAT).

Advantages of indirect taxes

People have an element of choice. They can avoid the tax by not buying the commodity.

The government can use the taxes to encourage or discourage spending on certain commodities.

Indirect tax does not have a disincentive effect on work and effort.

The taxes are unavoidable and even foreign tourists visiting Britain have to pay.

The taxes conform to most of the criteria of good taxation.

Disadvantages of indirect taxes

Indirect taxes are regressive because they are greater as a percentage of a low income than as a percentage of a high income.

They have an inflationary effect because they raise prices of commodities. Furthermore, this may encourage high wage demands.

Certain groups in society argue that they are heavily penalized (e.g. smokers, drinkers and car drivers).

The incidence of the tax can be shifted finally to the consumer, who is then faced with high prices.

(v) DIFFERENT TYPES OF DIRECT TAXES

Income tax (personal tax) . . . A tax levied on an individual's personal income and is paid as you earn (PAYE). It is automatically deducted from a person's wages/salary by the Inland Revenue. Each person has a personal allowance of tax-free income, which is not taxed. Then tax is imposed at a progressively higher rate (i.e. there is a higher percentage of tax on higher incomes). Economists often refer to the existence of the *poverty trap*, where an individual (a low-income earner) may become worse off by getting a job (or by getting a wage increase). This may happen because although he gains a higher income he may move into a higher tax bracket and may also lose allowances and supplementary benefits. Where the individual decides to remain unemployed rather than get a job, this is called the *unemployment* trap.

Capital gains tax A tax on the disposal of certain assets where the asset is sold for a profit. It is a progressive tax and is mainly applied to sales of securities and investment property. There are exceptions, such as the sale of the family home.

Inheritance tax (capital transfer tax) A progressive tax on gifts made at any time, including death. It applies only after a certain minimum amount. One exemption is capital left to a surviving spouse.

Corporation tax A proportional tax on the profits of companies. It is often criticized for discouraging investment in new capital and machinery because the company has less profit to spend. Companies in the assisted areas pay less corporation tax.

Wealth tax A tax which has never been introduced in Britain but is often proposed. It would be imposed on an individual's wealth, not income. There is a good deal of uncertainty about how it would operate – would it be paid once or annually? Would it be paid on farmlands? Who would assess the value of wealth?

Note: National Insurance contributions are not a type of tax but are compulsory payments by employers and employees to the government. They go to finance sickness and accident pay.

(vi) DIFFERENT TYPES OF INDIRECT TAXES

Customs duties Customs duties are dealt with in the section on international trade on pp.240–1.

Excise duties These are taxes imposed on certain commodities such as car tax, motor vehicle excise duty, petrol tax, wine and spirits duty, tobacco tax, etc.

Value Added Tax (VAT) This is the most important indirect tax and was introduced by the government in 1973. VAT is widely used in the European Economic Community (see p.255–6) and in 1973 Britain joined the EEC.

The VAT rate is decided by the government of the day and may easily be changed. Usually there will be a *standard rate* (at the beginning of 1987 this was 15 per cent) which applies to most commodities. It is imposed at each stage of the production and distribution process on the value added to the commodity. Credit is given for VAT already paid. Assume an example with a hypothetical VAT rate of 10 per cent.

£ Purchase price		£ Selling price before VAT	£ VAT liability	£ VAT credit	£ VAT to pay
0	Grower sells to producer	100	10	—	10
110	Producer sell to wholesaler	200	20	10	10
220	Wholesaler sells to retailer	250	25	20	5
275	Retailer sells to consumer	300	30	25	5

The consumer will have to pay £330 for this commodity.

Some commodities are *zero rated*, which means that a supplier can reclaim any tax levied on inputs when he purchased them; a children's clothes supplier, for example, can claim back any VAT he paid on the clothes and raw materials when he bought them. The consumer does not pay any VAT. Zero-rated commodities include basic foodstuffs, books, newspapers, children's clothes, drugs and medicines. They are zero rated mainly for social and cultural reasons.

Other commodities are *exempted* from VAT, which means that the commodity is not subject to VAT at the point of sale to the consumer but the supplier cannot reclaim any VAT on inputs (e.g. financial services, education and health).

(vii) THE EFFECTS OF TAXATION

Obviously the effects of the tax system depend on whether the government decides to raise revenue mainly by direct or by indirect taxation. It also depends on which individual taxes within these broad categories it decides to adopt.

Direct and indirect taxes will have differing effects on consumers' incomes, savings and investment, inflation, effort and economic performance. Refer to the advantages and disadvantages of direct and indirect taxes on pp.185–6.

MC2   Corporation tax is paid by a company on its
(a)   turnover
(b)   assets
(c)   floor space
(d)   imports
(e)   profits

MC3   An example of indirect tax is
(a)   corporation tax
(b)   income tax
(c)   rates
(d)   tobacco tax
(e)   capital gains tax

MC4   Which of the following taxes is most likely to be progressive?
(a)   Value Added Tax
(b)   car tax
(c)   inheritance tax
(d)   excise duties
(e)   tariffs

MC5   On which of the following taxes does the revenue earned by the government rise automatically with inflation?
(a)   tobacco tax
(b)   inheritance tax
(c)   motor vehicle tax
(d)   Value Added Tax
(e)   income tax

(b) THE BUDGET AND PUBLIC SECTOR BORROWING REQUIREMENT (PSBR)

The UK government rarely manages to finance all its expenditure by means of taxation and other receipts. The government has to borrow money by selling gilt-edged government securities (see p.225) to both British and foreign institutions and individuals. This amount of annual borrowing is known as the *Public Sector Borrowing Requirement*. The government has to pay holders of this debt interest, and interest payments have themselves become quite a sizeable component of government spending.

When government spending exceeds government revenues (as it usually does), this is termed a *budget deficit* and the deficit is financed by having a PSBR. The Thatcher Conservative government (1979–) has attempted to reduce the size of the PSBR, arguing that a high PSBR reflects a high level of government spending and leads to both inflation and high interest rates, both of which are harmful to the

British economy. It is argued that high interest rates have to be offered by the government on the gilt-edged securities to persuade lenders to purchase these securities. If the government is offering high interest rates, all other financial institutions follow suit (to be competitive) and high interest rates exist throughout the economy. This is harmful, because it will mean that businessmen cannot afford to borrow money to finance investment. Investment falls, and jobs will be lost as Britain becomes uncompetitive. Inflation is caused, it is argued, because the government stimulates the economy too much by having high government spending (and a high PSBR). There is too much demand in the economy and the result is inflation. Critics of the government state that attempts to reduce the size of PSBR are deflationary and have led to less demand in the economy and higher unemployment.

The government has a second budget strategy open to it. It could have a *budget surplus*, where government revenues exceed government expenditure. This has rarely been achieved since 1945. It would mean, of course, that there would be no PSBR at all. This would have a dramatic deflationary impact on the economy and would reduce the level of demand in the economy, resulting in lower levels of inflation but a much higher unemployment.

A third budget strategy would be to have a *balanced budget*, where government expenditure is equal to government revenues. Again there will be no PSBR.

4 RECENT FISCAL POLICY AND CRITICISMS OF THIS POLICY

The Thatcher Conservative government (1979–   ) is mainly in favour of indirect taxation and wishes to reduce the levels of direct tax. The main reasons for this are that indirect taxes do not have a disincentive effect on effort and they leave an element of choice with consumers. It is also argued that government spending and PSBR should be lower because they cause higher interest rates and inflation. The government should leave the economy more to the operation of market forces and keep interference to a minimum. Supporters of government fiscal policy argue that the government should place greater emphasis on the supply side of the economy (*supply-side economics*) by encouraging people to work harder and invest more. This can be partly achieved by low direct taxation, leaving people with more disposable income (i.e. money in their pockets). Lower direct taxation will also reduce the 'poverty trap' discussed on p.186, and again stimulate people to get work and work harder. Operating on the supply side of the economy will stimulate more people to find work, and economic growth will take off. Thatcher government policy is called the Medium-term Financial Strategy (MTFS). The fiscal policy thus outlined is combined with strict control over money supply (see pp.210–11).

Critics of government policy argue that this move towards indirect tax is regressive and cuts in direct tax are not the best way to create more jobs and stimulate economic growth and prosperity. If people are taxed less they will spend much of their increased disposable income on imports, and this will have an adverse effect in the balance of payments, the £ exchange rate and jobs. Critics argue that it is far better to raise money by taxes (mainly direct, which are not regressive or inflationary) to finance higher levels of government spending. These higher levels of government spending will set up a 'multiplier effect' (see p.183) and create jobs. The government must involve itself in the economy and directly operate on the demand side by expanding its own government spending. Inflation can be kept under control by some kind of prices and incomes policy (see pp.168–9).

The fiscal argument between the Thatcher government and its critics can be summarized by stating that the Thatcher government feels that the best way forward to create jobs is to keep inflation and direct taxation low. Critics argue for higher government spending. Lower direct taxes versus high government spending. What do you think?

MC6   A budget deficit is one
(*a*)   where public spending is less than the amount of revenue
(*b*)   where public spending is greater than the amount of revenue
(*c*)   where public spending is equal to the amount of revenue
(*d*)   where the budget leaves most taxpayers with less disposable income
(*e*)   where mistakes made by the government mean that government spending does not equal the amount of revenue

MC7   Which of the following fiscal measures would *not* increase demand in the economy?
(*a*)   less income tax
(*b*)   less VAT
(*c*)   less public borrowing
(*d*)   increased unemployment benefits
(*e*)   increased spending on pensions

MC8   Which of the following measures would the government take to finance its borrowing requirement?
(*a*)   sell gilt-edged securities
(*b*)   sell Bills of Exchange
(*c*)   sell ordinary shares
(*d*)   buy Treasury Bills
(*e*)   buy debentures

MC9   Which of the following will *not* tend to lead to greater equality of income distribution?
(*a*)   income tax rates

(b)   Value Added Tax
(c)   capital gains tax
(d)   inheritance tax (capital transfer tax)
(e)   unemployment benefits

MC10   Which of the following is not an instrument of fiscal policy?
(a)   interest rates
(b)   old age pensions
(c)   direct taxes
(d)   indirect taxes
(e)   government subsidies

EXTENDED WRITING QUESTIONS

1 (a)   Distinguish between central government revenue and local government revenue.
    (b)   (i) Examine the main sources of central government revenue.
           (ii) Examine the main items of central government spending.
    (c)   The government is undecided between reducing income tax or increasing public spending as a means to create more jobs in the economy.
           (i) How would jobs be created by each method?
           (ii) Discuss the advantages and disadvantages of each method.

2 (a)   What is meant by (i) fiscal policy and (ii) monetary policy?
    (b)   Why does the government levy taxes?
    (c)   In a particular year government expenditure is greater than government revenue.
           (i) What economic term describes this situation?
           (ii) What are the likely economic consequences of such a policy?
    (d)   Discuss the arguments for an increase in government spending.

3 A government has stated a preference for direct rather than indirect taxation. It also favours progressive rather than regressive taxation.
    (a)   Distinguish between:
           (i) indirect and direct taxation.
           (ii) progressive and regressive taxation.
    (b)   The government decides to increase the standard rate of Value Added Tax. Discuss the likely economic consequences of such a tax change.
    (c)   How could the government, through fiscal policy, reduce the inequalities in the distribution of income and wealth in the country?
    (d)   The government is considering giving grants to all those over the age of sixteen who stay on in full-time education. Identify two advantages and two disadvantages of such a policy.

4 (a)   Distinguish between (i) progressive taxation and (ii) regressive taxation.

(*b*)   With reference to the table below, state for each of the columns A, B, and C whether it illustrates (i) a progressive tax (ii) a regressive tax or (iii) a proportional tax in relation to gross income.

Gross income	Tax paid £		
£	A	B	C
40,000	400	4,000	10,000
20,000	400	2,000	2,000
10,000	400	1,000	200

(*c*)   Give reasons for your answer to part (*b*).

(*d*)   Analyse the likely economic effects of a reduction in the basic rate of income tax.

5   (*a*)   What is meant by
           (i) 'the poverty trap'?
           (ii) Public Sector Borrowing Requirement (PSBR)?

(*b*)   Why and how could the government attempt to reduce the 'poverty trap'?

(*c*)   Examine the objectives of government spending.

(*d*)   Why would a government attempt to reduce the size of the PSBR?

DATA RESPONSE 1   Newspaper extracts on the Budget, March 1986.

A CUT of one per cent in the basic rate of income tax is the big surprise in this year's Budget.

It comes down from 30 per cent to 29 per cent, and the Chancellor promised further cuts next year and the year after with the eventual aim of bringing the rate down to 25 per cent.

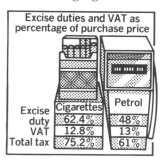

Source: *Daily Mail*

NEW INCOME TAX BANDS

OLD	NEW
Taxable Income*	Taxable Income*
Up to £16,200 ....30%	Up to £17,200 ....29%
£16,201 to £19,200 ......40%	£17,201 to £20,200 ......40%
£19,201 to £24,400 ......45%	£20,201 to £25,400 ......45%
£24,401 to £32,300 ......50%	£25,401 to £33,300 ......50%
£32,301 to £40,200 ......55%	£33,301 to £41,200 ......55%
£40,201 and over 60%	£41,201 and over 60%

Source: *Daily Mail*

(a)   (i) Give one example of a direct tax and one example of an indirect tax referred to in the newspaper extracts.

(ii) Distinguish between direct and indirect taxes.

(b)   Give two reasons why you think the proportion of tax in the purchase price of cigarettes and petrol is so high (75.2 per cent and 61 per cent respectively).

(c)   (i) Explain how the item of 'new income tax bands' indicates progressive taxation.

(ii) Why is Value Added Tax regarded as regressive?

(d)   Examine the likely economic consequences of a fall in the basic rate of income tax from 30 per cent to 29 per cent.

(e)   The Chancellor has increased taxation on cigarettes by 11p on a packet of 20. Examine the likely effects on:

(i) cigarette prices

(ii) taxation revenue gained from cigarettes

(iii) employment prospects in the tobacco industry.

Answer

(a)   (i) Direct tax: income tax (personal tax). Indirect tax: VAT or excise duty on petrol or cigarettes.

(ii) Direct tax is any tax on income and is collected by the Inland Revenue. Examples include income tax, inheritance tax, capital gains tax and corporation tax.

Indirect tax is any tax on expenditure on goods and services. VAT and any excise duty would be examples. Indirect tax is collected by the Customs and Excise Department.

(b)   (i) Good revenue-raisers because of inelastic demand.

(ii) The government may wish to discourage consumption of these products (for different reasons).

(c)   (i) Progressive tax occurs when higher income earners pay a greater percentage of tax. The bands illustrate this. High-income earners will have higher marginal and average rates of tax.

(ii) Any consumer purchasing a specific commodity will pay the same percentage VAT. However, the tax as a percentage of income will be greater for the poor man than for the rich. This illustrates regressive taxation.

(*d*) (1) Higher demand in the economy because people have more money (higher disposable income).

(2) Reflationary effects on jobs and prices.

(3) More money spent on imports.

(4) Stimulate more effort and more motivation (supply side economies).

(5) Reduces the 'poverty trap'.

(6) Larger PSBR.

Of course, much depends on the level of government spending and other taxes. My answer assumes that they remain unchanged.

(*e*) (i) Increase price by as much as 11p because of inelastic demand.

Most of the tax (if not all of it) will be passed on to consumers.

(ii) Cigarettes are a good tax revenue-raiser because of inelastic demand.

(iii) The demand for cigarettes tends to be inelastic but there may be some small drop in demand, reducing jobs in the tobacco industry.

DATA RESPONSE 2

PUBLIC MONEY, 1986-87

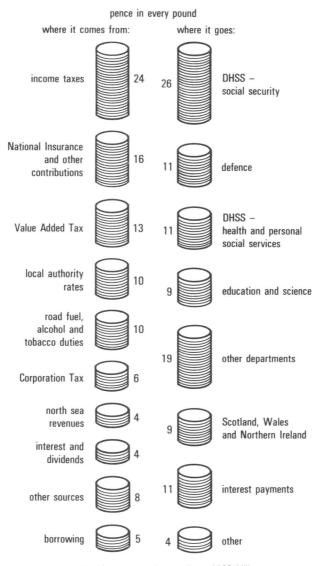

pence in every pound

where it comes from:			where it goes:
income taxes	24	26	DHSS – social security
National Insurance and other contributions	16	11	defence
Value Added Tax	13	11	DHSS – health and personal social services
local authority rates	10	9	education and science
road fuel, alcohol and tobacco duties	10	19	other departments
Corporation Tax	6		
north sea revenues	4	9	Scotland, Wales and Northern Ireland
interest and dividends	4		
other sources	8	11	interest payments
borrowing	5	4	other

cash totals of revenue and expenditure £163 billion

(*a*) (i) What is the largest source of government revenue in 1986–7?

(ii) What is the largest sector of government expenditure in 1986–7?

(*b*) Distinguish between National Insurance contributions and local authority rates.

(*c*) (i) Explain the meaning of borrowing as a source of revenue.

(ii) Explain how the government borrows money.

(d)   (i) Distinguish between a budget deficit and a budget surplus.

(ii) How large is the budget deficit in 1986–87?

(iii) Describe the main economic consequences of a large budget deficit.

Answers to multiple-choice questions:

MC1	(c)	**MC6**	(b)
MC2	(e)	**MC7**	(c)
MC3	(d)	**MC8**	(a)
MC4	(c)	**MC9**	(b)
MC5	(d)	**MC10**	(a)

MONEY, BANKS AND THE FINANCIAL SYSTEMS

CONTENTS

Contents

A study of money and banking is required by all GCSE syllabuses. The chapter is subdivided as follows:

1   **Money**
    Qualities of a good monetary medium.
    The functions of money.
    Stages in the development of money.
    Money in a modern economy.
    Credit cards.

2   **Commercial banks**
    What are commercial banks?
    The functions of commercial banks.
    Bank liquidity and profitability.

3   **The Bank of England**
    The Central Bank.
    The functions of the Bank of England.

4   **The creation of credit and monetary policy**
    How commercial banks create credit.
    Limits to this process of credit creation (monetary policy).

4   **Other Financial Institutions**

1 MONEY

(a) QUALITIES OF A GOOD MONETARY MEDIUM

If something is to be acceptable as a good monetary medium it should possess the following qualities:

(i) **Portability**: easily carries from place to place.

(ii) **Durability**: a long life, will not perish or wither away or be easily defaced.

(iii) **Divisibility**: easily divided into smaller amounts of money for small purchases.

(iv) **Acceptability**: accepted by people in the economy as having some value.

(v) **Scarcity**: it should be limited in supply.

(b) THE FUNCTIONS OF MONEY

Money should perform the following four functions:

(i) A MEDIUM OF EXCHANGE

Money acts as *the medium* between any exchange. For instance, workers will accept money for the labours they have performed and will use it to purchase a variety of commodities and services. In a modern economy, money allows specialization to take place since the workers know that they can use the money in order to satisfy their wants.

(ii) A MEASURE OF VALUE

Money overcomes the disadvantages of amounts encountered in barter. How many of X should be exchanged for how many of Y? This problem is overcome, since all commodities and services are given a value in terms of money which can serve as a standard for comparing the values of different commodities, etc.

(iii) A STORE OF VALUE

When a commodity is acceptable as a form of money, it can be stored. It is very convenient to hold wealth in this way. However, money may well lose its value if stored over a period of time, perhaps due to inflation (rising prices). This would mean that the monetary exchange value declines in terms of the commodities, etc, which can be purchased.

(iv) A MEANS OF DEFERRED PAYMENT

Money should be both acceptable and durable. This being so, the buyer may be able to defer payment for a short period of time. The seller will accept this arrangement because of confidence in the fact that money will still have value when payment is eventually made. This often applies in modern business negotiations when, say, a three-month period is granted before payment need be made (see pp.212–13 on Bills of Exchange). Of course inflation (or rising prices) may limit confidence in money as a means of deferred payment.

(c) STAGES IN THE DEVELOPMENT OF MONEY

Money has not always had the form which we know today. It could be anything which a society wishes to give value and accept as money. Some forms have not always conformed to the qualities mentioned previously.

(i) BARTER

Barter is the exchange of goods for other goods. This is used in relatively primitive societies. The disadvantages are that to work it depends on the 'double coincidence of wants' (when the two people exchanging goods both want the other item being offered). There is, however, the problem of amounts. How many of product X is worth how many of product Y? In a modern economy barter would not be a convenient form of exchange.

(ii) ONE COMMODITY USED AS MONEY

There have been many occasions when a particular commodity has been accepted as money. This normally occurs in undeveloped countries (for instance, seashells have been used in the South Pacific Islands). It can also occur in moments of economic collapse in advanced economies, e.g. the use of cigarettes in Germany in the hyperinflation of the late 1920s. There are therefore obvious drawbacks in using commodities as money.

(iii) COINS

As units of account, coins have been a good form of money. Originally they had value in themselves, since they were made from the precious metals of gold or silver. However, in Britain's modern economy the coins in use are made from alloys of copper, nickel and bronze and as such have no real value in themselves. Modern coins are called 'token coins'.

(iv) LEGAL TENDER

Legal tender refers to the fact that notes and coins of the Bank of England must be accepted in settlement of a debt in Britain. It also limits the amounts of coin which can be paid at any one time. (Notes issued by the Scottish banks are legal tender only in that country but are nevertheless usually accepted throughout Britain at their full face value).

(v) BANK NOTES

Bank notes have their origins in the receipts for deposits of valuables issued by goldsmiths in the seventeenth century. These receipts were used as a means of exchange and were acceptable as a method of payment. Before 1914 most Bank of England notes were convertible, in that they could be converted into gold. There is still written on these notes the words 'I promise to pay the bearer on demand the sum of [five] pounds', referring to the fact that the bearer is entitled to gold. In today's economy, however, this is a worthless statement because notes are inconvertible and cannot therefore be converted into gold. These notes and coins are often referred to as 'token money' because they have no real commodity value but are still accept as having money value. Currency is a term used to include bank notes and coins.

(vi) BANK DEPOSITS SUBJECT TO WITHDRAWAL BY CHEQUE

In recent times Britain has increasingly become a 'cashless society' in that most payments, especially business transactions, are made in the form of a cheque. It is important to note that a cheque itself is not money but a representation of it. The money is the bank deposit, whilst the cheque is merely a transfer order authorizing the transfer of money from one bank account to another. A cheque, however, is not legal tender and cannot be enforced in payment of a debt in the same way as bank notes or coins.

(d) MONEY IN A MODERN ECONOMY

Money is anything which is *generally acceptable* as a means of payments. This definition clearly includes notes and coins. It also includes bank deposits subject to withdrawal. There are other forms of payment which we can call near-money (or quasi-money) which are sometimes but not always acceptable like postal orders, Bills of Exchange and, most important these days, credit cards.

(e) CREDIT CARDS

Credit cards are a recent innovation which is becoming increasingly popular, particularly in the field of personal financial affairs. Examples include Access, Barclaycard and American Express. Credit cards have the following characteristics:

– A customer can make monthly purchases up to his/her credit limit – a figure agreed between the customer and the bank – thus saving on the use of cheques and possibly on bank charges as well.

– Credit card details are printed on to a receipt/voucher issued by the retailer and signed by the customer.

The top copy is kept by the customer as a receipt and record for checking with his or her statements.

One copy is kept by the retailer as a record of sale.

One copy goes to computer headquarters of the issuing organization.

Details of the purchase are recorded and added to the retailer's and customer's accounts.

– Once a month the computer centre sends the customer details of purchases and amount owing.

– The customer is obliged to pay a minimum proportion of the debt within the next month and payment is recorded by computer.

– If the customer pays all the debt within the month, his or her account is then clear and no interest is charged.

– If the customer pays none or part of the debt, the computer calculates how much interest is to be charged and this is added on to the next month's account.

– The monthly interest rate is thus calculated twelve times a year and the actual annual rate would be quite high. It is therefore an expensive way to borrow money.

MC1 Of all methods of payment, the only recognized legal tender is
(*a*)   cheques
(*b*)   bank notes/coins
(*c*)   cheques and bank notes
(*d*)   Bills of Exchange
(*e*)   bank notes and Bills of Exchange

MC2 Token coins are
(*a*)   not legal tender
(*b*)   valueless
(*c*)   worth less than the value of the metal they contain
(*d*)   worth more than the value of the metal they contain
(*e*)   none of these

MC3 Which of the following features of notes and coins indicate that they are legal tender?
(*a*)   they are relatively scarce
(*b*)   they are backed by gold
(*c*)   they are backed by government securities
(*d*)   they are issued by commercial banks
(*e*)   people are obliged by law to accept them in settlement of debt

2 COMMERCIAL BANKS

(a) WHAT ARE COMMERCIAL BANKS?

Commercial banks may also be called joint stock banks (because they issue shares), clearing banks (because they clear cheques) or high street banks (because they are situated mostly in the main or high street of towns). In essay questions commercial banks may be called by any of these alternative names.

There are four big commercial banks: Barclays, Lloyds, Midland

and National Westminster. However, there are other important commercial banks including the Royal Bank of Scotland, Clydesdale Bank, The TSB Bank, Coutts and the Co-operative Banks, with numerous branches throughout Britain.

The origins of the commercial banks are to be found with the goldsmiths of the seventeenth century, who accepted deposits of valuables and in return issued receipts which were the beginning of bank notes. The goldsmiths developed into private banks (no shareholders) and in turn developed into joint stock banks. Amalgamations have taken place over time, and today only a few large commercial banks remain.

(b) THE FUNCTIONS OF COMMERCIAL BANKS

(i) ACCEPTANCE OF DEPOSITS

When an individual opens an account with a bank this is regarded by the bank as a liability, since that money is owed by the bank to the depositor. There are two main types of account which can be opened:

Current account

The advantages of a current account are that money is secure; is repayable on demand; a cheque book is given and the holder therefore enjoys the advantages of cheques; the holder may use most of the services offered by the bank.

The disadvantage is that no interest is payable on money in the account – thus the customer should endeavour to keep the miminum balance in the account so as not to incur charges.

Deposit account

The advantages of a deposit account are that it receives a rate of interest on deposit balance (subjected to tax deducted at source) and the holder can deposit surplus funds at any time.

Depositors should, wherever possible, constantly review their balances in order to obtain the most effective rate of interest. Other alternative possibilities include building society term deposits, local authority loans, unit trusts, National Savings, etc. A great deal, of course, will depend upon the depositor's personal choice of accessibility of funds and his or her tax position.

The disadvantages are: no cheque book; the depositer will have to wait for a period of time (usually seven days) before withdrawing money; there is a restriction on use of the bank's other services; the rate of interest is often below the amount that may be obtained elsewhere.

(ii) MAKING LOANS

The making of loans is a highly profitable part of a bank's business. Loans are regarded by the bank as a profitable asset.

They are made in a variety of ways:

Creating a loan account (personal loans)

Here the customer has an agreed amount credited to his or her account. At the same time a loan account is debited with that same amount. The loan is repaid by regular fixed instalments out of monthly salary, etc. Interest is usually fixed and calculated on *the initial amount* borrowed, and is included in the repayments. It is therefore not as cheap as the overdraft when borrowing over a short period of time.

Granting an overdraft

An overdraft allows a customer to overspend, or withdraw, on his or her current account up to an agreed sum and for a given time. A rate of interest is charged on *the daily amount* borrowed and is therefore more economical than a loan account over a short period of time. The rate of interest will fluctuate depending on the prevailing interest rates at the time.

Issuing credit cards

The credit card system is mainly organized by the commercial banks.

It is worth noting that the government often dislikes this aspect of banks' activity since they have the power to create money, which may cause inflation. We discuss how banks do this and what the government does to restrict their ability to do so on pp.210–11.

(iii) ACTING AS AGENT FOR PAYMENT

Cheques

This method is used when the creditor knows or trusts the drawer (i.e. the person who writes the cheque) and is willing to accept his or her cheque. It may also be used when paying on an irregular basis.

Banker's order (or standing order)

A banker's order is used when a regular amount can be paid by the bank on authorization from the customer. Thus the bank saves the customer time and trouble in remembering to pay these regular bills and in addition saves the customer postage and correspondence. It is also a useful method of payment when sums such as insurance premiums have to be made at regular intervals (perhaps monthly).

Direct debits

These are similar to banker's orders (see above) but are authorizations by the customer for the bank to accept any amount from named persons or organizations for the debit of his or her account.

Bank Giro (or credit transfer)

Where a business has a number of creditors to pay monthly, it can avoid the cost and inconveniences or writing several cheques by using the Bank Giro.

The firm can make out one cheque covering the total of all payments, plus a list of creditors with details of account numbers and bank branches. Private customers can also use this service to pay their bills, such as gas, water, telephone, electricity, etc.

Banker's drafts

A cheques may not be acceptable to a creditor, especially if the drawer is not known. A banker's draft is in reality a bank cheque, signed by the bank's officials, drawn on itself and made payable to the payee (the person receiving the cheque). The drawer will at the same time write a cheque, drawn by him or herself, in favour of the bank. The creditor will therefore accept the banker's draft as being safe and secure. This method of payment is frequently used when the creditor will not accept the personal cheque of the drawer and needs more security, as in the case of a house sale or in international trade payments.

(iv) OTHER SERVICES PROVIDED BY BANKS INCLUDE

–   Issue of foreign exchange and travellers' cheques.
–   Investments: the bank may employ a firm of stockbrokers to buy or sell stocks and shares on behalf of its customers. It will also keep the securities safely and collect dividends for its customers.
–   Custody of valuables such as deeds, silver, jewellery, etc.
–   Night safes: businessmen can deposit cash after the bank has closed.
–   Cheque cards, status enquiries, cash dispensers, company registration.
–   Executor and trustee business: the administration of a dead person's estate may be taken on by a bank if so requested. In addition, specialist departments may undertake a private individual's tax returns and give advice on tax matters.
–   Factoring: the bank may agree to factor the debts of its client. It purchases the debts and in return has some responsibility in the running of the firm.

(c) BANK LIQUIDITY AND PROFITABILITY

Banks are faced with a difficulty about what proportion of assets to keep in profitable, but rather illiquid, form (i.e. they cannot quickly be turned into cash) and what proportion of assets to keep in not very profitable but liquid form (i.e. they can quickly be turned into cash). Banks need to keep some assets in liquid form to meet any unforeseen demands on them from depositors requiring their money back. If the bank was unable to meet depositors' requests, there might be a panic run on the bank and it would lose the confidence of depositors.

To resolve this difficulty banks keep a proportion of their assets in liquid but not very profitable forms. This is usually about 8–10 per cent. The rest can be kept in more profitable but illiquid form.

The liquid reserve assets include:

- holdings of Treasury Bills.
- holdings of Bills of Exchange.
- reserves held at the Bank of England.
- money at call with the Discount Houses (see p.212).
- holdings of government securities with less than twelve months left to mature.

In addition, the banks keep a proportion of assets in cash form in the tills.

The functions of commercial banks are an extremely important topic in the syllabus, and you should be prepared to answer questions similiar to the following:

MC4 My standing order at the bank means
(*a*) I can receive cash from my account without presenting cheques
(*b*) the bank will refer to me before paying cheques I have drawn
(*c*) I can overdraw my account up to an agreed figure
(*d*) the bank will pay on my behalf an agreed amount at agreed intervals until I cancel the order
(*e*) none of these

MC5 Which of the following is regarded as a liability by clearing banks?
(*a*) customer overdrafts
(*b*) personal loans
(*c*) direct debits authorized by customers
(*d*) money at call
(*e*) customer deposits

MC6 The most liquid asset of a commercial bank is
(*a*) cash in tills
(*b*) advances
(*c*) investments
(*d*) money at call
(*e*) overdrafts

3 THE BANK OF ENGLAND

(a) THE CENTRAL BANK The Bank of England is often called by examiners 'the Central Bank'; this is because it is at the centre of the British banking system. The Bank of England originated in 1694 when King William III wanted to raise money to fight the French. It developed into the most important private bank. In the Bank Charter Act 1844 its pre-eminence was established and Bank of England notes were to be the most important bank notes issued. In 1946 it was nationalized and at the present time keeps the principal government accounts and is therefore the government's bank.

(b) THE FUNCTIONS OF THE BANK OF ENGLAND

(i) NOTES ISSUE

The Bank Charter Act 1844 meant that the Bank of England was to become the main note-issuing bank in the country. Today the Bank of England has a monopoly in this, apart from the Royal Bank of Scotland.

(ii) THE BANKERS' BANK

The commercial banks use the Bank of England in a similar manner to customers using a commercial bank. The banks keep reserves at the Bank of England which, as we have seen, are used, among other things, to make payments after a day's clearing of cheques. These reserves are regarded by commercial banks as liquid assets.

(iii) EXTERNAL RESPONSIBILITIES

The Bank of England has close contact with the central banks of other countries. It provides services for other central banks, e.g. holding their reserves of sterling. International organizations such as the International Monetary Fund (see pp.256–7) and International Bank for Reconstruction and Development (see p.257) also keep some reserves with the Bank of England.

(iv) OPEN-MARKET OPERATIONS

Since 1981 this has been an important aspect of monetary policy (see p.210). Through open-market operations the Bank of England can influence the amount of money in circulation (see p.211) and the level of interest rates. The Bank aims to keep short-term rates of interest within an unpublished band, which it may change from time to time. Discount Houses, when they are short of funds, must now offer to sell acceptable bills to the Bank of England which the Bank will agree to take in exchange for cash only if the discount terms are within the unquoted band of interest rate. Hence the reluctance of financial institutions to borrow (i.e. sell securities) from the Bank of England unless absolutely necessary, i.e. the Bank is 'a lender of last resort'.

(v) THE GOVERNMENT'S BANK

This is a most important function of the Bank of England and includes:

Protection of gold and dollar reserves
The Bank determines the lending rate, administers government regulations as regards control of foreign exchange, and arranges loans to improve Britain's reserves.

Management of Exchange Equalization Account

If the pound is in danger of dropping in value in terms of foreign currencies and the government does not wish this to occur, the Exchange Equalization Account will purchase pounds, with foreign currency, on the exchange markets. More demand for pounds will increase the price of pounds (remember supply and demand analysis!) If the pound is rising in value, however, the government may require the Exchange Equalization Account to sell pounds to keep its value down. In this way the value of the pound is kept more stable over a short period of time, so assisting importers and exporters.

Management of the Exchequer Account

The Bank of England receives tax revenues into this account and administers government spending.

Management of the National Debt

The National Debt is the amount owned by the government to individuals and organizations both at home and abroad. Foreign governments may also hold some of the debt as their reserves. The debt consists of Government securities, both long- and short-term, issued by the Bank of England to help finance government spending. An important type of security is the *Treasury Bill*, which is a short-term loan to the government (three months) paying interest at the current rate. In addition the Bank of England organizes payment of interest on the National Debt.

Operation of the government's monetary policy

This is such an important function that we shall examine it in great detail in the next section. It should be noted at this point that monetary policy is concerned with the supply of money and the level of interest rates. This is different from *Fiscal policy*, which is government policy regarding the level of taxation, government spending and public sector borrowing. See Chapter 10 on Fiscal Policy.

4 THE CREATION OF CREDIT AND MONETARY POLICY

(a) HOW COMMERCIAL BANKS CREATE CREDIT

You should follow this analysis closely, especially as it is quite difficult to understand.

The money supply consists of notes and coins in circulation, and bank deposits. Of course, the government can create money itself by issuing more notes and coins. However, banks themselves can create money (or credit in this context), since they can create bank deposits. For the purpose of example we may assume that a bank makes a loan to a customer of £1,000. If the customer pays this to his or her creditor who is a customer of the same bank, the following situation has arisen:

Bank's liabilities	Bank's assets
deposits £1,000 (from customer)	loans £1,000 (to customer)

The bank has therefore created credit.

Of course, not every customer of the bank requires a loan – many keep their accounts in credit without having the need to overdraw, and large sums are kept on deposit. At an early stage in their development, banks realized that depositors would not require all their money back at once. All the bank was require to do was to keep back some of the deposits in reserve asset form to meet demands of depositors. The bank was therefore in a position to lend out the rest at interest.

As an example, assume that there is a 10 per cent reserve asset ratio (i.e. 10 per cent of deposits have to be kept in the form of liquid reserve assets). Thus, in its most sophisticated form, an initial deposit of £1,000 can support the creation of £9,000 of additional deposits.

Bank's liabilities		Bank's assets	
Initial deposit	£1,000	Reserve assets	£1,000
Created deposits	£9,000	Loans	£9,000
	£10,000		£10,000

In other words, the bank has treated all the initial deposit as reserve assets, enabling it to creat loans of £9,000. Reserve assets at £1,000 are 10 per cent of total deposits standing at £10,000. Thus the bank is confident that it can meet any demands on it by depositors.

(b) LIMITS TO THIS PROCESS OF CREDIT CREATION

The Bank of England and the government may sometimes wish to restrict the banks' ability to create credit because this is considered inflationary, since it will increase consumer demand. Too much demand may lead to increasing prices (inflation).

(i) In addition to the balances held at the Bank of England, the clearing banks are required to keep a further proportion of their deposits in short-term liquid assets (so-called minimum reserve assets). Thus they may satisfy the Bank of England that *adequate liquidity* is available.

(ii) GOVERNMENT MONETARY POLICY

A restrictionist monetary policy is created when the government – through its agent, the Bank of England – attempts to reduce money supply. The instruments of a restrictionist monetary policy include:

Open-market operations

The Bank of England sells securities (Government stocks and shares) on the open market. These are purchased by investors, who write cheques out to the Bank of England. The commercial banks' deposits at the Bank of England are reduced accordingly. This reduces the minimum reserve assets and the power of the banks to create credit.

Special deposits

The Bank of England may call in special deposits from the commercial banks. These are in addition to their reserves held at the Bank of England. This again reduces the power of the commercial banks to create credit.

Government directives

The government may issue directives through the Bank of England to stop creating credit. This may be to one particular sector of the economy or to the economy in general.

Funding

The Bank of England will sell long-term government securities. This is similar to open-market operations but extends over a longer period.

The Bank's lending interest rate

The Bank of England conducts its operations so as to keep short-term interest rates within an unpublished band. All other interest rates tend to follow its lead, making credit more expensive and therefore less attractive.

These are the weapons of monetary policy. As we have seen, a restrictionist monetary policy is introduced in an attempt to reduce inflation. On the other hand, an expansionist monetary policy (where the monetary weapons are used in the opposite way, e.g. a decrease in the Bank's lending interest rate) will be introduced in an attempt to increase employment and stimulate economic growth and output. A restrictionist monetary policy is sometimes called deflationary. An expansionist monetary policy is sometimes call reflationary. Why would the government wish to operate a reflationary monetary policy?

MC7 The Central Bank in Britain is called
(a)   Lombard Banking
(b)   The Midland Bank
(c)   The Bank of England
(d)   Lloyds Bank
(e)   Royal Bank of Scotland

MC8 Inflation means that money
(a)   rises in value
(b)   falls in value

(c)   is decimalized
(d)   becomes scarce
(e)   becomes larger in denomination

MC9   Open-market operations is the buying and selling of
(a)   ordinary shares by the commercial banks
(b)   government securities by the public corporations
(c)   government securities by foreigners
(d)   ordinary shares by nationalized industries
(e)   government securities by the Bank of England

MC10   When acting as lender of last resort, the Bank of England lends to the money markets through
(a)   Discount Houses
(b)   clearing banks
(c)   merchant banks
(d)   Stock Exchange
(e)   commercial banks

5. OTHER FINANCIAL INSTITUTIONS

(a) DISCOUNT HOUSES

The London Discount Market consists of ten Discount Houses. Their main function is to 'discount' a variety of bills, securities or 'promises to pay' issued by the government, local authorities, banks and industrial firms. Discounting is the process of buying a security for less than its face value and holding the security until it matures. The Discount Houses fulfil a very useful function, providing short-term funds which are always in great demand by both government and industry. They deal amongst other things in Bills of Exchange (see below) and Treasury Bills. Discount Houses also act as underwriters (i.e. they will purchase any surplus not taken up by the members of the money market) to the Treasury Bill issue.

Discount Houses need a great deal of capital to finance their activities. They receive money from deposits by the public, foreign sources, borrowings from the commercial banks and the Bank of England. The loans from the commercial banks are considered by these banks to be part of their easily redeemed assets and are termed 'money at call'.

For an analysis of how the Bank of England acts as 'lender of the last resort' to the Discount Houses, refer back to p.208.

(b) ACCEPTING HOUSES (OR MERCHANT BANKS)

Examples include Barings, Lazards and Rothschilds. The traditional business of Accepting Houses is the accepting of *Bills of Exchange*, which are widely used in the settlement of international debts. They are unconditional orders made by importers, accepting liability for the payment of money to exporters at an agreed future date. This means that for a commission, the Accepting House will guarantee that a bill will be paid on maturity. This means that the bill will be more easily discounted on the discount market. By endorsing the bill, therefore, the Accepting House guarantees payment of the bill should the drawer default. This is an important role, since it allows trade to take place between two firms (perhaps in different countries) who are not known to each other. The name of the Accepting House, however, will be known worldwide. (This aspect of their business is in decline, due largely to the reduced role of the commercial Bill of Exchange and competition from commercial banks in the business of overseas credit.)

Accepting Houses fulfil a wider role in that they control unit trusts (see p.204) and give financial advice to firms on investment management, on insurance and on sponsoring new capital issues. They also provide an expertise which is in great demand by foreign and British firms alike.

(c) ISSUING HOUSES

Issuing Houses specialize in the issue of new securities. Examples are Rothschilds and Morgan Grenfell. Many Issuing Houses also act as Accepting Houses. They arrange the public issue of stocks and shares on behalf of governments and firms. You should refer to p.221 for an analysis on the new issue market. Issuing Houses will underwrite a new share issue to ensure that all shares are taken up. They offer loans to companies and also offer advice on new issues regarding price of issues and numbers of shares to be sold.

(d) FINANCE HOUSES

Finance houses are a major source of medium-term finance (i.e. six months–five years), mostly in the form of hire purchase loans. (Hire purchase is used mainly to purchase consumer durables, especially motor vehicles.) They receive money in the form of deposits, mainly from commercial banks. Famous finance houses include United Dominion Trust, Lombard Banking and Bowaters.

(e) BUILDING SOCIETIES

Building societies advance mortgage loans with the main purpose of house purchase. These mortgage loans are repayable by instalments over many years and are subject to interest rates. These interest rates are an important economic and political indicator. Deposits come mostly from individuals and receive an interest payment. The biggest building societies include the Halifax, Abbey National and Woolwich.

(f) INSURANCE COMPANIES	Insurance companies collect huge sums of money from insurance premiums from clients insuring any risk which may happen. There are two main categories of insurance: life assurance and general insurance (fire and accident). Insurance companies invest by lending to government, in private investment projects and overseas.
(g) NATIONAL SAVINGS BANKS	This is operated in post offices and there are two main types of deposit – ordinary accounts and investment accounts. The latter pays a higher rate of interest but is subject to notice of withdrawal. The NSB hands its deposits over to the National Debt Commissioner to invest mainly in government securities.
(h) THE TSB BANK	The TSB Banks accept deposits and now offer cheque-book facilities. Most of their funds invested in government securities. The TSB Bank became a plc in 1986 and has become increasingly similar to a clearing bank.
(i) THE NATIONAL GIRO BANK	This is operated through post offices and the head office is in Bootle (Merseyside). Deposits can be made in cash at the post office, or cheques can be sent to Bootle in prepaid envelopes. Even non-members can pay into someone else's account. Members have cheque-book facilities for withdrawals and can cash cheques up to £50 at post offices. The Giro Bank offers most of the services of commercial banks including loans and overdrafts, standing orders and direct debits. They have the advantage of longer opening hours and Saturday opening.
(j) UNIT TRUSTS	A unit trust uses its funds to make investments during the period of the trust, which may be over many years. It is possible for an investor to purchase sub-units in the trust, thus allowing people of limited means to enjoy membership. A variety of securities are purchased and divided into units worth say £2,000. This money is then subdivided into sub-units of say £1 each, which are offered to the public. The investor is therefore in the same position as if he or she had bought a small holding in each of the securities which constitute the trust unit. The main advantage is that the unit holders are provided with a wide range of investments, so that risks are minimized.

(k) INVESTMENT TRUSTS

These are joint stock companies with limited liability. Investors buy shares in the trust, which then purchases securities in other companies. Profits made through buying and selling of these securities and dividends are divided amongst shareholders according to how many units they own.

EXTENDED WRITING QUESTIONS

1 (a) Define 'money'.
(b) Explain the functions performed by money in a modern economy.
(c) Outline the main forms of money in the UK.
(d) How is the amount of money regulated in the UK?

Answer

(a) Money is anything which is *generally acceptable* as a medium of exchange. The key phrase is 'generally acceptable'.
(b) To answer this you need to discuss the main functions of money:
– money as a medium of exchange
– money as a store of value
– money as a unit of account
– money as a measure of value
– money as a standard for deferred payments
Do not confuse the functions of money with the qualities possessed by money (i.e. it is durable, scarce, portable, etc.).
(c) The main forms of money in the UK are notes and coins of the Bank of England and bank deposits subject to withdrawal by cheque (note that the cheque is not money). Other forms of 'near-money' include credit cards and postal orders.
(d) The amount of money is regulated in the UK mainly by the government through its agent, the Bank of England. You need to discuss how clearing banks create more deposits and how the Bank of England regulates their ability to create deposits. Discuss the means of monetary control, such as interest rates. Open-market operations and special deposits. The Bank of England regulates the supply of money through its monetary policy. Moreover, no single clearing bank can go it alone and create money. If it does so, it will find that its reserves at the Bank of England will diminish after the day's clearing of cheques. The reserves at the Bank of England are regarded as a liquid asset which must be maintained.

2 (a) What is a clearing bank? Give two examples.
(b) What services are provided by a clearing bank for its customers?
(c) It is sometimes said that clearing banks create credit.

(i) Explain the meaning of this statement.

(ii) State the limits to this process of credit creation.

3　(a)　What is meant by the 'money supply'?

(b)　With the aid of an arithmetical example, show how commercial banks create credit.

(c)　Explain how the Bank of England can reduce the level of bank lending by using

(i) open-market operations

(ii) special deposits.

4　(a)　Distinguish between (i) a central bank and (ii) a clearing bank.

(b)　Explain the advantages which a small firm can enjoy by being a customer of a clearing bank.

(c)　What are the functions of the Bank of England which make it so important?

5　(a)　Compare a National Giro account with a current account of a commercial bank.

(b)　What part is played by the Discount Houses in the UK financial system?

(c)　Explain the role played by Issuing Houses in the new issue market.

DATA RESPONSE　　The following table refers to the assets and liabilities of a clearing bank.

	£ million
Customers' deposit accounts	80
Customers' current accounts	120
Notes and coins in tills	10
Investments	70
Advances to customers	80
Treasury Bills	14
Money at call	12
Balance at Bank of England	10
Special deposits	4

(a)　What is a clearing bank? Give two examples.

(b)　From the list above give

(i) two of the bank's assets

(ii) two of the bank's liabilities.

(c)　What is the total value of (i) the assets and (ii) the liabilities of the clearing bank?

(d)　In the list above name the bank's

(i) most liquid asset

(ii) most profitable asset.

(e)　How do banks attempt to reconcile profitability with liquidity?

Answers to muliple-choice questions:

MC1	*(b)*	**MC6**	*(a)*
MC2	*(d)*	**MC7**	*(c)*
MC3	*(e)*	**MC8**	*(b)*
MC4	*(d)*	**MC9**	*(e)*
MC5	*(e)*	**MC10**	*(a)*

THE STOCK EXCHANGE

CONTENTS

Contents

The Stock Exchange is popular with examiners. This chapter has been subdivided into the following sections:

1 **The meaning of the Stock Exchange** What is the Stock Exchange? Examples of Stock Exchanges. The Unlisted Securities Market (USM).

2 **Why do investors buy securities?** The security will earn a dividend and yield. The security may increase in price.

3 **How the Stock Exchange works** Brokers and market-makers. How shares are bought and sold.

4 **Types of securities traded on the Stock Exchange** Government stock or bonds. Local government stock or bonds. Shares. Debentures.

5 **Speculation on the Stock Exchange** Bulls. Bears. Stags.

6 **The price of securities** Factors which may cause share prices to change. The official list. The Financial Times Stock Index.

7 **The advantages and disadvantages of the Stock exchange.**

1 THE MEANING OF THE STOCK EXCHANGE

(a) WHAT IS THE STOCK EXCHANGE?

The Stock Exchange is a type of market where dealings in government stocks, public company shares and similar types of **securities** take place. It provides the means whereby buyers and sellers of stocks and shares, etc., can carry out their necessary exchanges. In other words, it is largely a market for securities that have already been issued. It is important for you to note that not all stocks and shares of public companies are sold on the Stock Exchange. When stocks and shares are first issued they may be sold in one of the following ways on what is called the *new issue market:*
(i)   by Issuing Houses to the general public acting as agents for the company;
(ii)   entirely to Issuing Houses, who will later sell them to the general public or large institutions such as insurance companies;
(iii)   placed with particular shareholders;

(iv)   offered to existing shareholders and the general public.

As a result, when the person or institution that first bought the securities wishes to sell them at later date, they will be sold on the Stock Exchange.

(b) EXAMPLES OF STOCK EXCHANGES

The London Stock Exchange is the most important exchange in Britain and forms part of a network which includes a number of exchanges in other cities throughout Britain, such as Bristol, Manchester and Glasgow.

(i) THE STOCK EXCHANGE IN LONDON

Dealings in stocks and shares began in Britain in the second half of the seventeenth century with the growth of joint stock companies. The buying and selling of shares took place in numerous London coffee houses. Eventually Old Jonathan's Coffee House and then the New Jonathan's Coffee House became the centre of dealings and the first real Stock Exchange. Today the Stock Exchange is housed in a twenty-six-storey building in London which was opened in 1973.

(ii) THE STOCK EXCHANGES IN OTHER BRITISH CITIES

Stock Exchanges in Britain are divided into units, but closely linked in almost every respect to the London Exchange. For example, the Scottish Unit in Glasgow links with the one in London. Dealers in these Stock Exchanges have detailed knowledge about local company shares and are also members of the London Stock Exchange.

The importance of the London Exchange can be seen in its dealings with securities from all over the world. It is in close contact – by means of telephone, telex and cable – with all major Stock Exchanges abroad, including Paris, New York and Tokyo.

(c) THE UNLISTED SECURITIES MARKET (USM)

This market was opened in 1980 and is for small/medium-sized companies that do not wish for a full quotation on the Stock Exchange but do wish to sell a small percentage of their shares. The owners of the company retain control but obtain extra finance.

---

2 WHY DO INVESTORS BUY SECURITIES?

You should be aware that securities are bought for two reasons:

| (a) THE SECURITY WILL EARN A DIVIDEND AND YIELD | If a share bought for £1 earns a 10 per cent dividend (i.e. 10 pence) the dividend, or yield, received by the investor is also 10 per cent. If a £1 share is bought for £2, however (assuming its market price has increased), it will still earn a 10 per cent dividend (i.e. 10 pence) but its yield will be only 5 per cent. In other words, |

$$\text{yield} = \frac{\text{Nominal value (original or par price) of share} \times \text{dividend}}{\text{Market value of share}}$$

| (b) THE SECURITY MAY INCREASE IN VALUE | Shares bought today may be sold at a higher market price in the future. In the above example the £1 shares have been sold for £2 because there is a demand for them from other investors. As the number of shares issued by the company in question is fixed, the price of each share will increase. On the other hand, the £1 share above may fall in value to, say, 50p – particularly if the company has not made any profits or its prospects are poor. |

It is most important for you to know that it is not only private individuals who buy shares. Most securities are bought by institutional investors such as insurance companies, pension schemes, trade unions and commercial banks.

MC1 A Stock Exchange is
(*a*)   a central market for buying and selling all kinds of goods
(*b*)   a place where any business can borrow money from the members
(*c*)   a place where a register is kept of all public and private limited companies
(*d*)   a central market for buying and selling all kinds of securities
(*e*)   none of these

MC2 A shareholder receives a dividend of 10% on the shares which he purchased for £300. The nominal value of the shares is £200. The amount of his dividend is
(*a*)   £10
(*b*)   £20
(*c*)   £30
(*d*)   £50
(*e*)   £60

MC3 When some shares in a limited company have a face value of £100 and a market value of £95
(*a*)   the company has made a trading loss
(*b*)   the shares are said to be at a premium
(*c*)   the stockbroker and jobber between them lose the £5 difference when they sell the shares

(*d*)   the capital of the company remains the same despite a fall in the value of the shares

(*e*)   the market price is greater than the par price

3 HOW THE STOCK EXCHANGE WORKS

(a) BROKERS AND MARKET-MAKERS

After 1986, in what was called the 'Big Bang', the traditional role of 'stockbrokers and stockjobbers' was replaced by a new system of '*broker-dealers*'.

There are two types:

(i) THOSE WHO CONTINUE THE ROLE OF THE BROKER ACTING ON BEHALF OF THEIR CLIENTS

–   They buy and sell to the market-makers, acting in their clients' interests.

–   They arrange the transfer of shares, the registration of the change of ownership, and obtain share certificates.

–   they advise customers regarding investments and send price lists and prospectuses to clients.

(ii) MARKET-MAKERS WHO DEAL NOT ONLY AS BROKERS BUT ALSO AS DEALERS IN SHARES

–   They tend to specialize in one kind of security.

–   Market-makers can be found on the Stock Exchange floor. They deal only with brokers.

–   Market-makers make a profit by buying at a low price and selling at a higher price. The difference is the '*dealer's turn*'.

(b) HOW SHARES ARE BOUGHT AND SOLD

For the purpose of expediency, suppose an investor wishes to buy some shares from a well-known company.

(i) The investor contacts a broker (his or her bank manager may arrange this), giving precise details of how many shares are to be purchased.

(ii) The broker contacts a market-maker about the shares which the investor wishes to purchase, not revealing whether it is a buying or selling transaction.

(iii) The market-maker gives two prices. The low price is the one at which 'he' is prepared to buy. The high price is the price at which 'he' is prepared to sell. If the broker is not satisfied he will go to another dealer for a further quotation.

(iv) When both broker and market-maker agree, they both make a note of the purchase and the bargain is checked the next day. Each party will always honour the bargain, hence the motto of the Stock Exchange, 'My Word is My Bond'.

(v) The broker sends the client a contract note showing the purchase price of the share, the broker's commission, the amount of contract stamp duty (a duty or tax to the government), the amount of the transfer stamp (again a government duty).

(vi) Until the settlement day arrives, the client does not pay any money. Settlements take place on specified days and not at any other time. There are twenty-four settlement days in the year, most two weeks apart. An investor may therefore receive up to fourteen days' credit before he or she pays if the previous settlement day has just passed.

(vii) Settlement of deals is largely completed by a computer network known as Talisman and is concerned with the recording and movement of shares between buyers and sellers. (Should an investor wish to sell shares on the Exchange, the broker will sell the shares to the market-maker at an agreed price and eventually pay the investor the amount due.)

4 TYPES OF SECURITIES TRADED ON THE STOCK EXCHANGE

You should know that it is not only the shares of public companies which are bought and sold on the Stock Exchange. There are other types of securities bought and sold, such as:

(a) GOVERNMENT STOCK OR BONDS

The government issues stocks and bonds to finance its expenditure. They pay a fixed rate of interest and repayment is guaranteed. They are considered to be safe because they are backed by the government and given the name 'gilt-edged securities'. Bonds are usually issued in units of £100 at a fixed rate of interest and repayable or redeemed by the government on a particular date, e.g. 8 per cent Savings Bonds repayable 31 December 1999. Stock is a type of loan and can be divided into any quantities, e.g. £438.21 of stock could be bought.

(b) LOCAL GOVERNMENT STOCK OR BONDS

These are issued by local authorities to help finance long-term spending on local rather than national projects, the benefits of which will be felt for many years (e.g. swimming pools). Again, such investments are very safe, carrying a fixed rate of interest and guaranteed repayment. See pp.112–13 on ways in which local authorities raise finance.

(c) SHARES

There are many types of share. A detailed account can be found on pp.96–8 in the chapter on private enterprise. A knowledge of the different types of share is essential to the answering of many questions. Blue-chip shares are the ordinary (or equity) shares of highly regarded public companies.

(d) DEBENTURES

These are similar to bonds but are issued only by joint stock companies. See p.98.

5 SPECULATION ON THE STOCK EXCHANGE

Many of the transactions on the Exchange are for investment purposes. However, some investors are speculators and they purchase and sell securities with a view to making quick profits. There are three types of speculators, known as bulls, bears and stags, and you should know the meaning of each of these terms. Be prepared to answer questions on speculation.

(a) BULLS

A bull is an optimist who will buy shares in the hope they they will rise in prices before the next settlement day. He or she could make a profit in the following way:

(i) Shares are purchased and the usual contract not is made out. No money is due before next settlement day.

(ii) In the meantime the shares have risen in value – the bull therefore immediately sells them at the new but 'higher' price but receives no money before next settlement day.

(iii) The settlement day arrives. The bull receives the sum from the sale of shares, paying for those bought. After paying the broker's commission, the remainder is profit.

(b) BEARS

A bear is a pessimist who will sell shares in anticipation that they will fall in price before next settlement day. He or she could make a profit in the following way:

(i) The bear sells shares he 'does not have' but receives no money before the next settlement day.

(ii) Before next settlement day the price of the share falls, then he or she will buy at the new lower price.

(iii) On settlement day the shares now in his or her possession are sold at the previously agreed higher price. After paying the broker the commission, what is left is profit for the bear.

(c) STAGS

When new issues of shares take place, the public may be invited to apply for them. Very often these are oversubscribed (i.e. more people want the shares than there are shares available) and the market price of the share will rise.

A stag will anticipate such an oversubscription and will buy as many of the shares as possible as quickly as possible with a view to selling them at a higher price later. If the market price of a new security is higher than the issue price, the difference is the *premium*. If it is lower, the difference is the *discount*.

Speculators are often criticized for bringing about the price movement they want by acting together. For instance, bulls may act together and start buying shares in a particular company. This will cause prices to rise and they will then sell these shares (making a profit); the price will subsequently fall and they will buy them back again.

6   THE PRICE OF SECURITIES

(a) FACTORS WHICH MAY CAUSE SHARE PRICES TO CHANGE

Like any other price, the price of shares is determined by the supply of and demand for that share. If there is little demand for the share, its price is likely to fall. On the other hand, if the demand increases then the price of the share will rise. Demand and supply could be influenced by:

(i)   **The annual results of the company** Particular attention will be paid to the balance sheet to see how much profit the company has made and how much of this profit is distributed in dividends to shareholders.

(ii)   **Rumours and newspaper articles** about the company in particular or the market in general.

(iii)   **Other factors** Share prices tend to go up or down, reflecting the general economic and political situation. For instance, if Britain's unemployment is rising, inflation is at a high level and there is a great deal of industrial unrest, the share prices will probably fall until a more stable situation exists. In other words, outside factors such as a war in a certain 'sensitive' part of the world would cause share prices to fall rapidly because of the lack of confidence in the national or world economic situation.

(b) THE OFFICIAL LIST

Each unit (or section) of the Stock Exchange publishes a daily Official List containing the names of securities in which they deal as well as the latest prices. The Stock Exchange Daily Official List is published in London and contains the names and prices of nearly 10,000 quoted securities; an abridged version of the Official List appears in the leading financial papers (especially the *Financial Times*).

(c) THE FINANCIAL TIMES STOCK INDEX

(i) The FT-SE 100 share index Refer to index numbers on pp.164–5 and understand how index numbers operate. The FT-SE 100 share index is reported every evening (on TV and radio) and published in the following day's newspapers. It is an average measure of the price movements of 100 key and leading ordinary shares. The base year is 1935 and it is given the index number 100.

(ii) The FT-SE 30 share index This is the average measure of thirty 'blue chips' (first-class ordinary shares), again using 1935 as the base year with an index number of 100.

Movements in both indices indicates how the Stock Exchange behaved on a particular day. It is closely watched by analysts, investors and dealers as a base to form opinions about future share price movements.

MC4 Gilt-edged stock is
(*a*)   government stock
(*b*)   stock in gold mines
(*c*)   stock which has risen in value
(*d*)   foreign stock
(*e*)   stock which is worthless

MC5 Blue chips are
(*a*)   government securities
(*b*)   first-class ordinary shares
(*c*)   founders' shares
(*d*)   debentures
(*e*)   first-class preference shares

MC6 Which of the following would not be sold on the Stock Exchange?
(*a*)   shares in public companies
(*b*)   local government bonds
(*c*)   stocks in nationalized industries
(*d*)   foreign stocks
(*e*)   shares in private companies

MC7 A 'bull' is a speculator who
(*a*)   buys shares at lower prices hoping to selling at higher prices
(*b*)   sells shares now and hopes to buy at lower prices in the future
(*c*)   buys new issues

(d)   buys gilt-edged securities
(e)   buys only blue chips

7 THE ADVANTAGES AND DISADVANTAGES OF THE STOCK EXCHANGE

(a) DISADVANTAGES

It is often said that the Stock Exchange is nothing more than a casino where speculators can force the price of shares up or down to satisfy their own desires for profits. There have been periods in the history of Stock Exchanges when shares have risen because of speculation only to suffer disastrous declines later, e.g. the Wall Street (New York's Stock Exchange) crash in 1929.

(b) ADVANTAGES

There is no doubt that speculation does take place on the Stock Exchange, but the financial institutions and most private investors look on their holdings more as long-term investments than as a way of making a fortune overnight. The Stock Exchange performs a number of useful functions:

(i) It provides a market for share buyers and sellers and enables companies and governments to raise funds.

(ii) It encourages people to invest in stocks and shares because they know they will be able to sell these securities when they wish; their money will not be locked away for ever.

(iii) It enables people who wish to invest in companies to spread their money around. This way they avoid the risk of putting all their money into a company which ceases to trade and goes into liquidation.

(iv) Some of the speculation may be useful because market-makers are experts on share movements. If share prices are falling too low, dealers may buy them up and stabilize prices.

(v) It advertises share prices, allowing the public to follow their investments and change them as necessary.

(vi) It protects the public against fraud. If a share appears on the Official List it is almost a guarantee of honesty, since the firm will have been investigated by the Stock Exchange Council.

(vii) It is a 'barometer' of the health and well-being of the economy. If prices fall sharply on the Stock Exchange this probably reflects a general lack of confidence by investors and is soon noted by all other sectors of the economy.

MC8 Which of the following is not put forward as an advantage of the Stock Exchange?
(a)   it is a place where the government can raise capital

(b)   it encourages the purchase of more shares
(c)   it encourages speculation in share-buying
(d)   it is a barometer of the economy
(e)   it is a place where local authorities can raise capital

MC9 A person who buys shares on the Stock Exchange hoping that their price will fall is known as:
(a)   an optimist
(b)   a bull
(c)   a stag
(d)   a shareholder
(e)   a bear

MC10 Which of the following can be used to calculate the yield of a share?

(a) $\dfrac{\text{nominal value} \times \text{dividend}}{\text{market price}}$

(b) $\dfrac{\text{nominal value} \times \text{market price}}{\text{dividend}}$

(c) $\dfrac{\text{market price} \times \text{dividend}}{\text{nominal value}}$

(d) $\dfrac{\text{nominal value} + \text{dividend}}{\text{market price}}$

(e)   none of these

EXTENDED WRITING QUESTIONS

1 (a) Give two differences between ordinary shares and preference shares.
(b) (i) Distinguish between the market price of a share and the nominal price of a share.
(ii) Why might these two prices differ?
(c) Explain how the existence of the Stock Exchange makes it easier for companies to raise finance.

Answer

1 (a) Ordinary shares carry a vote at the AGM, have a variable rate of interest and are at the back of the queue to be paid out of profits.
Preference shares do not carry a vote, have a fixed rate of interest and have priority above ordinary shares to be out of profits.
Choose any two differences.
(b) (i) The market price of the share is the current price and is determined by supply and demand at any one time. The

nominal (or par) price is the initial price of the share when it was first issued.

(ii) They may differ for several reasons. The market price is determined by supply and demand for the share. This price will be influenced by factors specific to the company such as profits and expected profits, dividends paid and expected to be paid, rumours, and any factor affecting the firm's profitability.

The price of the share may also fluctuate due to general factors such as economic and political developments in the wider economy, e.g. the level of unemployment, inflation, the pound and interest rates.

(c) The Stock Exchange is a market for second-hand securities. Therefore shareholders know that they can buy and sell securities on the Stock Exchange at any time. Thus the Stock Exchange provides a market whereby buyers and sellers can always contact each other. The Stock Exchange also provides information whereby shareholders can follow share prices. This gives shareholders confidence and they purchase shares, enabling firms to raise finance.

2 (a) Why can the London Stock Exchange be described as an organized market?

(b) Distinguish between (i) the Stock Exchange and (ii) the new issue market.

(c) 'In the USA the number of shareholders swelled from 6½ million in 1952 to 43 million in 1984. In Britain numbers fell from 2½ million to about 1¾ million.'

(i) Explain this statement. Give reasons.

(ii) How is it proposed to widen share ownership in the UK?

3 (a) What is meant by speculation?

(b) Describe the activities of speculators on the Stock Exchange.

(c) 'The Stock Exchange is a market for second-hand securities.' Explain the meaning of this statement.

(d) Explain why the Stock Exchange is useful to some private enterprise companies.

4 The main function of the Stock Exchange is to act as a market for securities.

(a) What is a market?

(b) Why is this function so important?

(c) Indicate the main types of securities referred to in the above statement.

(d) Explain how securities are bought and sold on the London Stock Exchange.

5 (a) Using an arithmetical example, distinguish between (i) percentage dividend and (ii) percentage yield received from share ownership.

(b) Why is the percentage yield of more significance to the investor than percentage dividend?

(c) Why are so many different types of security traded on the Stock Exchange?

(*d*)   What factors may determine the price of shares
          (i) in a particular company?
          (ii) in general for all quoted companies?

Decision today on Chunnel prospectus delay

Flood of new issues may hit Eurotunnel funding

Source: *The Guardian*

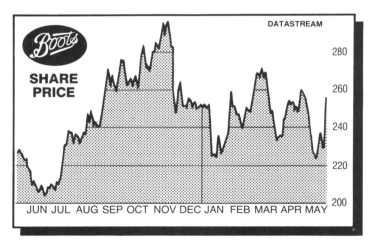

Source: *The Guardian*

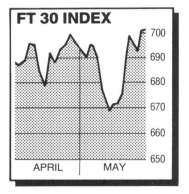

Source: *The Observer*

A BADLY wounded **pound** demoralised shares and **gilts** yesterday.

The **FT 30 share index** plunged 27·4 points to 1,309·9. The slump wiped £4,400m from share values.

Gilts were hammered unmercifully with falls of up to £2.

Sterling's suffering stemmed from sagging **oil** prices and worries that the chances of lower interest rates had evaporated.

Source: *Daily Mail*

(a)   (i) What are gilts?
    (ii) Describe four different types of security (not including gilts) which are dealt with on the Stock Exchange.
(b)   (i) What are 'new issues'?
    (ii) Explain three methods by which new issues are sold.
(c)   (i) What is the FT 30 Index?
    (ii) What factors may cause the FT 30 Index to fluctuate?
(d)   Give reasons for the Boots share price fluctuating during this period.
(e)   'The Stock Exchange is little more than a casino.' Do you agree with this statement? Give reasons for your answer.

Answer to multiple-choice questions:

MC1	(d)	**MC6**	(e)
MC2	(b)	**MC7**	(a)
MC3	(d)	**MC8**	(c)
MC4	(a)	**MC9**	(e)
MC5	(b)	**MC10**	(a)

FOREIGN EXCHANGES AND BALANCE OF PAYMENTS

CONTENTS

Contents

This chapter deals with international trade, which is a topic of major importance in all GCSE syllabuses, and you should expect examination questions to be set. The topic is subdivided into the following sections:

1 **International trade and protection** What is international trade? The advantages of international trade. How countries decide which commodities to produce (specialize in). Trade restrictions or protection. Why are trade restrictions introduced? When protection might not work.

2 **The terms of trade.**

3 **The balance of payments** Terms used in balance of payments statistics. How has Britain performed in its balance of payments in recent years? Britain's imports and exports: the pattern of trade.

4 **Balance of payments deficits and surpluses** The problem of a balance of payments deficit. The problem of a balance of payments surplus. How a balance of payments deficit can be corrected. How a balance of payments surplus can be corrected.

5 **Exchange rates** Fixed exchange rates. Floating exchange rates.

6 **The institutions of international trade** The European Community (the Common Market). The International Monetary Fund. (IMF). The International Bank for Reconstruction and Development (IBRD or World Bank). The General Agreement on Tariffs and Trade (GATT).

1 INTERNATIONAL TRADE AND PROTECTION

It is essential that you are aware of the importance of trade, and in particular the importance of international trade. You should also know the arguments in favour of restricting trade in favour of protection.

(a) WHAT IS INTERNATIONAL TRADE?

International trade is concerned with the buying and selling of commodities between the different countries of the world. Some countries, such as the USA and USSR, could provide most of the produce they need themselves; other countries, including Britain, rely heavily on other countries for their supplies of foodstuffs and raw materials.

(b) THE ADVANTAGES OF INTERNATIONAL TRADE

(i) Many countries do not produce enough food to feed their populations. Home-produced foodstuffs have to be supplemented by imports (purchases from abroad). For instance, Britain will import tea, coffee and wines.

(ii) Countries such as Britain cannot supply enough raw materials to support their industries. For instance, Britain can no longer produce iron ore to satisfy the steel industry. Thus the ore has to be imported from countries with a surplus, such as Spain and Sweden.

(iii) A large number of jobs depend on the export (selling to other countries) of goods and services. Many manufactured goods produced in Britain – such as cars, lorries, buses and refrigerators – are sold abroad. Also, many foreign countries involved in trade use British ships, aircraft, banks and insurance companies. Without international trade much of this employment would be lost.

(iv) International trade means a larger market for home-produced commodities.

(v) International trade means more competition and brings the advantages of competition such as more efficiency (see p.82).

(vi) International trade means a larger market and commodities have to be produced on a large scale. This brings the economies of scale (see pp.75–7).

(vii) The prosperity of all countries depends on their ability to sell goods abroad and purchase products which perhaps they cannot produce themselves. If international trade did not exist, people in all countries would suffer a lower standard of living. Consumers enjoy more variety and choice of commodities.

(viii) International trade means that countries specialize in producing a few commodities. Specialization has its advantages; see pp.57–8.

(ix) Political advantages: international trade is beneficial because through trading with other countries friendship and understanding will result. This is why, in recent years, Western Europe has attempted to increase trade with Eastern Bloc countries and China.

It is a measure of the importance of international trade to Britain that – despite being small in area and having less than 2 per cent of the world's population – it is the world's fifth largest trading nation (behind the USA, West Germany, Japan and France).

(c) HOW COUNTRIES DECIDE WHICH COMMODITIES TO PRODUCE (I.E. TO SPECIALIZE IN)

(i) A COUNTRY CAN PRODUCE SOME COMMODITIES BUT NOT OTHERS

This may be due to difference in climate or the distribution of raw materials. For instance, Britain is unable to grow oranges or mine gold and therefore has to import these commodities.

(ii) A COUNTRY CAN PRODUCE ONE COMMODITY BETTER THAN ANOTHER COUNTRY, AND VICE VERSA

Country A may be able to produce a commodity better than Country B; Country A therefore decides to specialize in this commodity. Country B may be able to produce another commodity better than Country A; Country B therefore decides to specialize in this other commodity. After specializing (or concentrating) in producing the commodity to which each country is best suited, the countries will decide to trade with each other. Britain, for instance, can produce wine, but perhaps not as cheaply or in such quantities as France. Therefore Britain will import most of the wine it requires, mainly from France.

(iii) A COUNTRY CAN PRODUCE BOTH COMMODITIES BETTER THAN ANOTHER COUNTRY

A country may be able to produce two commodities better than another country. However, it will decide to produce only the commodity in which its comparative advantage is greatest and allow the other country to produce the other commodity. This is called the Theory of Comparative Costs.

Example:

| | Output per person | |
	Oranges	Lemons
Country A	1	2
Country B	3	4

Here we can see that Country B has the absolute advantage in producing both oranges and lemons.

But what does each country have to give up if it specializes in producing just either oranges or lemons?

	Oranges given up to produce one lemon	Lemons given up to produce one orange
Country A	½	2
Country B	¾	1⅓

Here Country A has the comparative advantage in the production of lemons, because to produce a lemon Country A has to give up ½ an orange, whereas Country B has to give up ¾ of an orange. It is much better for Country A to produce lemons than for Country B to do so, because it has to give up less. Why does Country B specialize in oranges?

After deciding in which commodity they have a comparative advantage, each country will specialize in the production of that good; the production of both oranges and lemons will increase, trade will take place and people in both countries will enjoy a better standard of living.

Despite these arguments in favour of free (or international) trade, there have been several put forward in favour of restricting trade.

(d) TRADE RESTRICTIONS OR PROTECTION

Trade restrictions are implemented by governments to discourage international trade. There are several methods of protection for you to learn:

(i) TARIFFS (IMPORT DUTIES) OR CUSTOMS DUTIES

This is a type of tax placed on certain commodities imported into the country. Tariffs may be levied on an ad-valorem basis (i.e. as a percentage of value), or on a percentage of value), or on a specific basis (i.e. as an amount per unit). Thus if a car was imported worth £4,000 and the ad-valorem tariff was 10 per cent, the tax would raise £400; if the car increased in price to £5,000, the tax would raise £500. Tariffs serve two purposes: they raise money for the government and raise the price of imports, thereby reducing the quantity of imports.

(ii) IMPORT QUOTAS

This is a direct restriction on the quantity of imports allowed into a country. It is a more certain way of reducing imports, but on the other hand raises no tax. Nevertheless, this method of controlling imports is necessary in certain instances, for example drugs are imported on a quota basis only through certain ports or airports in Britain.

(iii) SUBSIDIES

This occurs when Britain's domestic (home) production is subsidized (or given finance) which allows it to sell at lower prices. So when importers try to compete with British domestic producers, they will find that their goods are more expensive and therefore demand for imported goods will be lower.

(iv) EXCHANGE CONTROLS

If an importer wants to purchaser commodities for import, he or she may do so by using the currency of the exporting nation. So if a government wishes to restrict imports it will restrict the availability of foreign currencies. Exchange controls were abolished in Britain in 1979.

(v) EMBARGO

This is a straightforward ban on trading with another country and is usually for political reasons.

(vi) DISCRIMINATION

By the domestic government in favour of home products, e.g. the Central Electricity Generating Board may be instructed to buy British coal even though foreign coal may be cheaper.

(vii) HEALTH AND SAFETY REGULATIONS

So designed purposely to keep out imports.

(viii) VOLUNTARY EXPORT RESTRAINT AGREEMENTS

Where two countries agree to limit the volume of exports to each other.

(e) WHY ARE TRADE RESTRICTIONS INTRODUCED?

Now that you know what the different weapons of protection are, you need to know the reasons why they may be introduced.

(i) TO CORRECT A BALANCE OF PAYMENTS DEFICIT

Normally, if Britain exports less than she imports, a balance of payments deficit (or loss) is the result. This means that more money goes out of the country to pay for imports than comes in from foreigners paying for Britain's goods. Tariffs and other such restrictions will in the short term discourage imports and correct Britain's balance of payments.

(ii) TO PROTECT INFANT INDUSTRIES

A country may be trying to build up a new industry. Such an industry could not survive if it was expected to compete with the imports of countries already established in that industry.

(iii) TO PROTECT DECLINING INDUSTRIES AND SAFEGUARD JOBS

Certain industries in Britain, such as textiles, are in decline. One of the main reasons for this is that foreign imports are cheaper and consumers do not buy British goods. Making imports more expensive could help Britain's declining industries and maintain jobs.

(iv) THE PREVENTION OF 'DUMPING'

Some foreign firms may choose to dump their surplus production in Britain and sell it at a price just high enough to cover costs or give a very small profit. This may be below the prices of British producers and drive them out of business.

(v) TO PROTECT STRATEGIC INDUSTRIES

Certain industries are so important that – in case of an international crisis, for instance – they must not be allowed to decline or die. Example would include agriculture, steel, shipbuilding and coal mining.

(vi) TO PROTECT JOBS

By protecting domestic industry, jobs are also safeguarded.

MC1   A duty which is based on the percentage of the price of goods is known as
(*a*)   ad-valorem duty
(*b*)   specific duty
(*c*)   percentage duty
(*d*)   a tariff
(*e*)   excise duty

(f) WHEN PROTECTION MIGHT NOT WORK

Protection may not be successful in achieving its objectives for the following reasons:

(i) BRITISH CONSUMERS MAY STILL PURCHASE IMPORTS

Even if tariffs have been put on them to make them more expensive, certain necessities may still be bought as imports, e.g. foodstuffs and raw materials. Such commodities have inelastic demand. Thus the balance of payments will not be helped.

(ii) OTHER COUNTRIES MAY RETALIATE

If Britain prevents imports entering this country, other countries may prevent British goods entering their country. Again the balance of payments will not be helped.

(iii) INEFFICIENT INDUSTRIES ARE PROTECTED

Perhaps restrictions are just protecting inefficient industries anyway, and these industries will eventually decline and die in the face of competition.

(iv) PROTECTION DOES NOT CONFORM TO THE THEORY OF COMPARATIVE COSTS

The advantages of international trade are lost.

2 THE TERMS OF TRADE

This measures the rate at which one country's commodities are exchanged against those of other countries. It is measured by comparing a country's export prices against import prices. If there is a relative movement in favour of export prices this means that for a given quantity of exports the country can purchase a larger quantity of imports, and its terms of trade have improved.

The terms of trade are measured by the formula:

$$\frac{\text{Index of average export prices}}{\text{Index of average import prices}} \times 100$$

The base year will have an index value of 100 and any movement in future years above 100 shows that the terms of trade have improved.

For an analysis of the way index numbers operate see pp.164–5, which deal with the Retail Price Index.

Many students become confused between terms of trade, balance of trade and balance of payments. The balance of trade and balance of payments are dealt with in detail on pp.244–5. Another source of confusion is whether an improvement in the terms of trade will always improve the balance of payments. The answer is that it depends on the elasticity of demand for exports and imports. An improvement in the terms of trade means that export prices are relatively higher and, given inelastic demand for exports, foreigners will continue to purchase much the same amount, revenues from exports will improve and so too should the balance of payments.

Terms of trade average (1980 = 100)

1970	103.9	1982	99.8
1975	87.6	1983	99.1
1980	100.0	1984	98.3
1981	101.0		

3 THE BALANCE OF PAYMENTS

An understanding of balance is essential in our study of international trade. Your also need to know the meaning of the balance of trade, the meaning of terms such as current account, visibles, invisibles and investment and other capital flows. You need to be able to distinguish these terms from one another and to understand their inter-relationship.

The balance of payments is a record of transactions between countries involved in international trade in one year. It is a record of receipts from exports and spending on imports. If a country's receipts are greater than its expenditure, it will have a balance of payments surplus. If a country's receipts are less than its spending, it will have a balance of payments deficit. Countries obviously prefer to be in surplus on their balance of payments because this means that they are earning more than is being spent in international trade.

Balance of Payments Statistics for Great Britain

£m	Visible balance	Invisible balance	Current balance	Official financing
1970	−34	+857	+823	−1,420
1975	−3,333	+1,810	−1,523	+1,465
1980	+1,361	+2,116	+3,477	−1,372
1981	+3,360	+3,569	+6,929	+687
1982	+2,055	+2,868	+4,923	+1,284
1983	−1,165	+4,411	+3,246	+816
1984	−4,255	+4,879	+624	+1,321
1985	−2,068	+5,020	+2,952	+927

(a) TERMS USED IN BALANCE OF PAYMENTS STATISTICS

(i) THE CURRENT ACCOUNT

This is divided into two parts:

Visible trade balance

This includes the imports and exports of goods. The difference between these is called the balance of (visible) trade. These figures are publicized each month and must not be confused with the balance of payments proper.

Invisible trade balance

This includes the import and export of services such as aviation; interest, profits and dividends; shipping; tourism; banking and insurance and the government services. Here are some examples:

If an American company uses a British ship to transport its goods from the USA to Brazil, this is an invisible export because they have paid for the use of that British ship with American money.

If Britain maintains an embassy in West Germany, this is an

invisible import (on government services) because staff are paid wages, etc., and that money is spent not in Britain but in West Germany.

If a British company with a factory in New Zealand earns interest, profits and dividends on its investment, this is an invisible export because that money enters Britain to pay for British shareholders.

The balance of visible trade and the balance of invisible trade are taken together and make up the balance on current account.

(ii) INVESTMENT AND OTHER CAPITAL FLOWS

This includes the import and export of capital for investment purposes. If capital flows into Britain because foreign firms or governments have purchased stocks or shares or built a factory, then this is regarded as an export because money has been transferred from abroad into Britain. On the other hand, if capital leaves Britain because British firms or the government have purchased foreign stocks or shares or built a factory abroad, this is regarded as an import because money has flowed out of Britain.

In future years, of course, those investments abroad may earn interest, profits and dividends for British companies and this would mean an inflow of money on invisibles.

(iii) THE BALANCING ITEM

It is not always possible to keep an accurate record of balance of payments because of errors and omissions. However, the Bank of England can see what is actually happening by changes in the official reserves it holds. A negative balancing item means that the balance of payments has been overvalued. A positive balancing item means that the balance of payments has been undervalued.

The current account balance plus the balance on investment and other capital flows plus the balancing item gives the *balance for official financing*, which is the balance of payments figure in reality. However, there is one more section of the accounts to describe.

(iv) OFFICIAL FINANCING

The balance of payments always balances. This refers to the fact that every penny of a deficit must be financed by borrowing or running down reserves of foreign currency. Likewise, every penny of a surplus must be allocated to paying off loans or adding to reserves of foreign currency. The reserves of gold and foreign currency are kept by the Bank of England. Borrowing is mainly from the IMF (see pp.256–7).

(b) HOW HAS BRITAIN PERFORMED ON ITS BALANCE OF PAYMENTS IN RECENT YEARS?

(i) VISIBLES

In the early years of the 1980s Britain did well on the visible part of current account. Generally Britain's exports in terms of value were more than the value of imports. What reasons can be put forward?

–   The relatively lower price of British goods due to higher rates of inflation in some foreign countries.

–   Increased trade with Common Market countries.

–   Britain sells a large volume of high-quality North Sea oil to overseas markets (particularly Europe), accounting for a substantial surplus on visible trading items. The contribution of North Sea oil revenues has been a major positive influence on visibles and the balance of payments.

The decline of manufacturing trade

The surplus on visibles gave way in the mid-1980s to a deficit. This may be explained by the decline in oil prices, leading to a fall in the value of Britain's oil exports. Also, there was a deficit on manufacturing trade during the mid-1980s for the first time since the Industrial Revolution of the early nineteenth century.

Causes of the decline in manufacturing trade:

–   A relatively high value of the pound in the mid-1980s made British exports uncompetitive and imports relatively cheap.

–   High British interest rates led to a decline in investment in British manufacturing.

–   The world recession caused a decline in British manufacturing.

–   Deflationary government policies (both fiscal and monetary) have damaged British manufacturing. The government's main aim was to cure inflation by deflationary policies.

–   In terms of quality, British manufactures are inferior and less value for money than foreign manufactures. This criticism is often levelled at the British car industry.

–   Prices are still higher for British manufactures than for foreign manufactures. This may be due to inefficiency, low productivity (see p.123) and high wages.

The decline in the British manufacturing sector is very worrying. This is because traditionally Britain has been known as a manufacturing country, and one day the oil will run out. However, some economists argue that Britain will build up its service sector (e.g. banking, insurance, finance, etc.) and this will to some extent compensate for the manufacturing decline.

(ii) INVISIBLES

There has always been a surplus on Britain's invisible transactions taken as a whole. This includes the banking and insurance services of the City of London, together with profits on other services provided

BRITAIN'S WINNERS AND LOSERS

TOTAL DEFICIT £4.1bn | TOTAL SURPLUS £5.036bn

VISIBLE TRADE

£m

Food, beverages & tobacco	–£3,527
Basic materials	–£2,852
Oil	£7,137
Other fuels/ lubricants	–£1,547
Semi manufactures	–£138
Finished manufactures	–£3,647
Other	£474

INVISIBLE TRADE

£m

Sea transport	–£1,151
Civil Aviation	£469
Travel	–£448
Financial/ other services	£6,038
Interest/profit/ dividends	£4,586
Government transactions	–£4,295
Private transfers	£163

Source: *Daily Mail*

by Britain to the rest of the world. The surplus on invisibles is always a very important positive factor in the balance of payments.

(iii) INVESTMENT AND OTHER CAPITAL FLOWS

This may vary from year to year, depending to a large extent on comparative interest rates between London and other world financial centres, political pressures, market trends, etc.

(c) BRITAIN'S IMPORTS AND EXPORTS: THE PATTERN OF TRADE

This is an important section on what goods Britain imports and exports. It is a popular essay topic with examiners.

(i) THE GOODS WHICH BRITAIN IMPORTS AND EXPORTS

Analysis of visible trade 1984 by commodity

	Exports (% share)	Imports (% share)
Food and drink	6.7	10.4
Crude materials and oils	2.8	6.0
Fuels	21.8	11.9
Chemicals	11.7	12.9
Manufactures	24.1	27.1
Machinery and transport equipment	30.5	30.1
Other	2.4	1.6
	100	100

Recent changes in Britain's imports and exports

Imports In terms of value, the importation of crude oil was before 1980 the largest single item in Britain's imports. However, this has been severely reduced following the discovery and exploitation of North Sea oil and gas. In addition, recent years have seen a sharp rise in total imports of manufactures, reflecting higher demand for these products and machinery, etc., particularly from Japan.

There has also been a decline in the proportion of imported food-stuffs, largely due to the greater output of Britain's farmers.

Exports The largest share is taken by high-quality finished manufactures, which account for nearly half the total (e.g. electronic products, engines, vehicles, books and sports equipment). Semi-manufactures are the next most important category of exports.

Oil and chemical exports have become increasingly important, due to North Sea oil. Britain has since 1980 been an net exporter of oil, and it makes a significant contribution to balance of payments. Exports of textiles, metals and coal have diminished. Foodstuffs account for roughly the same proportion of exports as in previous years.

Analysis of visible trade 1984 by area

	Exports (% share)	Imports (% share)
EEC	44.8	44.7
Other Western Europe	12.4	16.8
North America	16.2	14.0
Other developed	5.2	7.1
Latin America	1.3	1.9
Middle East and North Africa	8.8	3.5
Other developing	8.8	9.1
Centrally planned economies	2.3	2.6

Recent changes in countries from whom we import and to whom we export

There are three major changes:

Britain's trade with her partners in the Common Market has increased markedly over the last few years.

Trade with the rest of Western Europe has also expanded over the same period.

Trade with the members of the Commonwealth such as Australia, Canada and India is proportionately less important now than ten years ago.

Trade with the USA (though still important) has also declined as a proportion of total trade in recent years.

4 BALANCE OF PAYMENTS DEFICITS AND SURPLUSES

(a) THE PROBLEM OF A BALANCE OF PAYMENTS DEFICIT

A balance of payments deficit is undesirable if it occurs year after year and is consistently large.

– It may lead to a fall in gold and foreign currency reserves (see p.245). If these disappear, the country will not be able to pay for imports and may have to stop trading.

– The country will have to borrow from the IMF (see p.257) and repay the loans with interest.

– It indicates that the economy is inefficient, that prices are too high and that the quality of domestically produced goods is poor. There is something wrong with the economy.

– A balance of payments deficit is regarded as a bad indicator of the economy. Measures may have to be taken, such as protection or deflation, which may have bad side effects.

(b) THE PROBLEM OF A BALANCE OF PAYMENTS SURPLUS

A surplus is usually regarded as desirable but may be undesirable if the surplus is made year after year and other countries are suffering deficits. These other countries may have to limit future trade by introducing protection or deflationary measures. Also, the surplus may be inflationary as more money flows into the economy, demand will increase and prices will rise.

(c) HOW A BALANCE OF PAYMENTS DEFICIT CAN BE CORRECTED

When a country makes a deficit on balance of payments it will try to remedy this in one of the following ways:

(i) BORROWING

To finance the deficit on balance of payments the country may have to borrow, usually from the International Monetary Fund (see p.257) or from other countries. This is only a short-term measure of help, and the deficit may appear again.

(ii) IMPOSING TARIFFS AND OTHER METHODS OF PROTECTION

This may be attempted but it may not work, and it does have its disadvantages – particularly retaliation by other countries.

(iii) DEFLATIONARY POLICIES

Deflation means attempting to reduce home demand, thereby keeping prices down and leading to less demand for imports. Such a policy may include

Deflationary monetary policy
This may include:

Increasing interest rates The government may raise interest rates, which will cause all other interest rates to rise. This will attract money into Britain, on investment and other capital flows.

Preventing banks from creating credit Banks may give people loans which they use to purchase imports and also cause prices to rise. If the government restricts the banks from doing this, imports will fall. For further details see the banking section.

Hire purchase restrictions By imposing restrictions such as larger deposit requirements, etc., hire purchase could be made more difficult and expensive to obtain. Again, this would lessen imports.

Deflationary fiscal policy
This may include:

Higher taxes Taxation could be increased. Thus consumers would have less money in their pockets with which to buy imports.

Lower government spending This would reduce the amount of demand in the economy and reduce import.

Deflation has the undesirable side effect of worsening unemployment in the British economy. Demand deflates, not only for foreign goods but also for British goods.

(iv) CURRENCY DEVALUATION

If the country is operating a system of fixed exchange rates (where a country's currency has a fixed value in comparison to other countries; see pp.253–4), e.g. £1 = $2, then it may choose to devalue the value of its currency against other currencies. This would make imports more expensive, therefore fewer imports will be bought; it would also mean that exports are cheaper and in consequence more exports will be made.

Example
    Before devaluation: £1 = $4   After devaluation: £1 = $2
Assume that Britain wants to export a car worth £10,000 to the USA: before devaluation the Americans had to spend $40,000 (10,000×$4) on the car. After devaluation, they will have to spend $20,000 (10,000×$2). Given the right conditions, it is hoped that more exports will be sold in the USA because the price is lower.

What will happen to the price of American imports to Britain? There are disadvantages, and devaluation may not work because:
−   The Americans may not buy more British goods even if they have become cheaper. This implies inelastic demand for British goods. Also, given inelastic demand, British consumers may continue to buy expensive foreign imports.
−   Other countries may also devalue their currencies and make their exports cheaper. This cancels out the effect of Britain's devaluation.
−   Britain may not be able to produce the number of cars that the USA requires because of strikes. This means that supply of British goods is inelastic.

– Because of the higher price of imports, it may cause inflation in Britain. This will, in the long run, make British export prices higher.

(v) ALLOWING THE POUND TO FLOAT DOWNWARDS

A country may not keep its currency fixed to another currency, as on a fixed exchange rate. It may allow its currency to float downwards; this would have the same effect as a devaluation. Britain has had a floating pound since 1972; before that she tried to keep a fixed exchange rate.

(d) HOW A BALANCE OF PAYMENTS SURPLUS CAN BE CORRECTED

A balance of payments surplus can be remedied by employing opposite measures to those used to correct a deficit. Instead of devaluation of currency a revaluation will be required on fixed exchange rates or an upward float on the floating exchange rate system. Instead of deflationary measures, reflationary policies will be required such as lower interest rates, encouraging bank credit and making hire purchaser easier. Protectionist measures will be reversed.

MC2 Which of the following items in the balance of payments account are invisibles?

 (i) imports of motor vehicles
 (ii) aviation
 (iii) tourism
 (iv) private investment overseas
 (v) interest, profits and dividends

(*a*) (i), (ii) and (iii)
(*b*) (ii), (iii) and (iv)
(*c*) (ii), (iv) and (v)
(*d*) (ii), (iii) and (v)
(*e*) (i), (iii) and (v)

MC3 In what section of the balance of payments would an increase in overseas investment in the UK be recorded?

(*a*) private transfers of money
(*b*) investment and other capital flows
(*c*) invisible imports
(*d*) interest, profits and dividends
(*e*) balance of trade

Match the definitions given MC4–6 with the terms lettered A–E. Each letter may be used once, more than once or not at all.

(*a*) The surplus on current account is less than the deficit on investment and other capital flow account.

(*b*) Visible exports exceed visible imports.
(*c*) The surplus on invisible items exceeds the deficit on visible items.
(*d*) Imports exceed exports and re-exports.
(*e*) The deficit on investment and other capital flows is less than the surplus on current account.

MC4 A current account surplus

MC5 A visible trade surplus

MC6 A surplus on balance of payments

MC7 Concerning Britain's international trade, which of the following is not true?
(*a*) the largest import, by value, is foodstuffs
(*b*) the largest export, by value, is manufactured goods
(*c*) Britain usually has a favourable invisible balance
(*d*) Britain's trade with the Common Market countries is increasing
(*e*) Britain is a member of the IMF

MC8 Which of the following is not an invisible item in the balance of payment figures?
(*a*) the cost of carrying mail for foreign countries
(*b*) charges for freight carried by aircraft
(*c*) charges for passenger travel by sea
(*d*) expenditure on machinery imported
(*e*) dividends payable to foreign shareholders

MC9 A country's visible balance is the difference between the
(*a*) volume of goods imported and exported
(*b*) value of capital goods exported and imported
(*c*) volume of consumer goods imported and exported
(*d*) value of goods imported and exported
(*e*) value of goods and services exported and imported

MC10 The following figures relate to a country's dealings with other countries in a particular year:

	£m
Imports of goods	1,000
Exports of goods	900
Invisible imports	4,000
Invisible exports	3,500

That country's balance of trade is

(a)   £500m deficit
(b)   £100m deficit
(c)   £100m surplus
(d)   £500 surplus
(e)   £400m deficit

5 EXCHANGE RATES

The exchange rate of the pound is the external value of the currency in respect of other countries' currencies. Exchange rates between currencies are necessary so that countries can purchase foreign currency and engage in international trade. A country needs foreign exchange to buy imports. There are two main systems of organizing exchange rates:

(a)   fixed exchange rates
(b)   floating exchange rates.

(a) FIXED EXCHANGE RATES

(i) MEANING

Exchange rates are fixed between currencies and government must make sure that the exchange rate remains fixed. A good example was the gold standard (used in the international economy up to 1914 and between 1925 and 1931) when currencies were fixed in terms of gold. Between 1945 and 1971 a system of *managed flexibility* existed, where exchange rates could be adjusted only between very narrow limits. The system was supervised by the IMF (see p.257).

(ii) HOW THE STERLING EXCHANGE RATE WAS FIXED

The government's agent, the Bank of England, operated the *Exchange Equalization Account* (see p.209). Also, *exchange controls* restricted the selling of pounds and buying of foreign currency (see p.241). The Bank of England was able to control the demand and supply of pounds and therefore the price of pounds (i.e. the exchange rate). Exchange controls were abolished in Britain in 1979.

(iii) ADVANTAGES OF FIXED EXCHANGE RATES

–   Certainty about the exchange rate encourages businessmen to trade. They know exactly how much each currency is worth in terms of other currencies.
–   Speculators cannot force the exchange rate up or down to make profits.

–   Government is encouraged to avoid balance of payments deficits, which would result in a drain on gold and foreign currency reserves (see p.245) and unpopular deflationary measures having to be taken.

Thus the government adopts a disciplined economic approach to avoid inflation and too many imports being sucked in.

(iv) DISADVANTAGES OF FIXED EXCHANGE RATES

Governments (e.g. in the UK), when faced with a balance of payments deficit, would initially have to employ a number of unpopular measures such as *protection or deflation* to protect the balance of payments. This might lead to higher unemployment and a lack of economic growth. However, the real problem might be an overvalued currency, making exports more expensive and imports cheaper. Given elastic demand, the high pound would be the main cause of the deficit on balance of payments.

Despite efforts to keep the value of the currency fixed, the government might eventually have to change the value of the pound. In the case of consistent deficits, a *devaluation* would be required. Devaluation is discussed in detail on p.250. In the case of consistent surpluses, a *revaluation* would be necessary.

A devaluation makes exports cheaper and imports more expensive (see p.250). Given elastic demand for exports and imports, the value of exports increases and the value of imports decreases – thus the balance of payments problem is corrected. A revaluation has the opposite effect.

(b) FLOATING EXCHANGE RATES

(i) MEANING

Floating exchange rates occur when the currency fluctuates up or down and finds its own price, depending on the demand and supply of the currency. Many factors will determine the price of the currency, not least the balance of payments situation. For instance, a balance of payments deficit means that a country exports less than it imports, the demand for its currency will be less than the supply and the price of the currency will fall.

Since 1972 the pound has floated. In reality there has been a system of 'dirty floating' in which, given a dramatic increase or decrease in the price of pounds, the Bank of England will intervene to influence the price.

(ii) ADVANTAGES OF FLOATING EXCHANGE RATES

The main advantage of floating exchange rates is that it *automatically* corrects a balance of payments deficit (or surplus). For instance, a balance of payments deficit will mean less demand for pounds (foreigners demand fewer pounds they are not purchasing British exports). The price of the pound will fall, exports will become cheaper and imports will be more expensive. This should, given elastic demand, increase the value of exports and reduce the value of imports. The balance of payments deficit will be automatically corrected.

(iii) DISADVANTAGES OF FLOATING EXCHANGE RATES

–   They lead to uncertainty amongst businessmen about the value of currencies and may lead to a fall in trade, because they are unwilling to enter contracts.

–   Speculators find it possible to operate to force currencies up or down and make profits for themselves by buying at low prices and selling at higher exchange rates.

–   Government economic policy may be undisciplined because it will consider that the balance of payments problem will automatically be corrected by an exchange rate adjustment. Therefore government could reflate or expand the economy with too much demand. Inflation will result.

MC11   Which of the following would *not result from a fall in the value of the pound?*
(*a*)   exports become cheaper
(*b*)   imports become more expensive
(*c*)   inflationary pressures decline
(*d*)   foreign holidays become more expensive
(*e*)   assuming elastic demand for exports, an increase in the value of exports

MC12   If the demand for pounds exceeds the supply of pounds in a system of floating exchange rates,
(*a*)   the pound exchange rate will remain the same
(*b*)   the supply pounds will decline
(*c*)   the pound exchange rate will rise
(*d*)   the pound exchange rate will decline
(*e*)   the pound will be devalued

6   THE INSTITUTIONS OF INTERNATIONAL TRADE

(a) THE EUROPEAN COMMUNITY (THE COMMON MARKET)

You have probably heard of the Common Market or European Community. You should know what it is, its aims and objectives, how it is controlled and the arguments for and against Britain's membership.

(i) ORIGINS AND MEMBERSHIP

The EC was formed in 1958 by the Treaty of Rome. It originally consisted of six founder members: Belgium, Luxembourg, The

Netherlands, France, West Germany and Italy. In 1973 three other countries joined: Britain, Eire and Denmark. Its objectives are full economic, monetary and political union between the member countries.

By 1979 some of these aims had been achieved, including the abolition of tariffs within the area (a common external tariff exists), a common agricultural policy, greater co-operation in fields of transport, law reform, etc. In 1981 Greece also joined, and Portugal and Spain joined in 1986.

The European Community is an example of a customs union where member countries have free trade amongst each other but a common tariff against non-members. A customs union is different from a free trade area (e.g. European Free Trade Association, EFTA), where countries have free trade with each other and there is no common tariff against non-members.

(ii) THE ADVANTAGES AND DISADVANTAGES OF EC MEMBERSHIP TO BRITAIN

Britain joined the Common Market in 1973 after two previous attempts to join had failed. The following are some of the arguments put forward for and against Britain's continued Common Market membership:

Advantages
Opens up a wide market with a very large population (c. 350m).

There are no tariff barriers between members. The advantages of free trade.

The members of the EC have all enjoyed a high rate of economic growth and improvements in their standard of living.

Britain's position in the world was becoming less important – by joining with other European countries she maintains an important voice in world affairs. This a political argument.

Most of Britain's trade is with the EC.

Competition should encourage British firms to become more efficient.

Disadvantages
Britain's contribution to the community budget is often greater than any aid she receives.

The Common Agricultural Policy has meant that food prices are higher than before.

Britain has lost her very close links with the Commonwealth countries such as Australia and Canada.

Britain has lost a great deal of her independence and control over her own affairs. This is a political argument.

Since British agriculture is highly efficient, much of the agricultural budget fund is spent on the inefficient farms abroad.

(b) THE INTERNATIONAL MONETARY FUND (IMF)

The IMF was set up at the Bretton Woods Conference in 1944. It consists of 130 countries who each contribute a quota of money to a fund. The size of the quota depends on the country's economic size. The IMF has six main objectives:

– To prevent balance of payments disequilibrium (i.e. large deficits and surpluses) between countries.

– To lend money to countries with balance of payments deficit problems.

– To eliminate exchange controls and restrictions.

– To promote exchange rate stability.

– To promote the growth of international trade.

– To promote international monetary co-operation and provide a forum for discussing trade problems.

The IMF has attempted to encourage more world trade by issuing more world finance through Special Drawing Rights (SDRs), which may be lent to borrowing countries and have to be accepted by other members. This has helped deficit countries pay their trade debts.

(c) THE INTERNATIONAL BANK FOR RECONSTRUCTION AND DEVELOPMENT (THE IBRD OR WORLD BANK)

The World Bank is a group of the wealthier world countries who seek to help less developed countries. It makes loans to governments and their agencies. Loans are intended to help poor countries to achieve some measure of economic growth. Emphasis is placed on education, agriculture, transport and energy schemes. The loans may be for very long periods and carry little or even no interest.

(d) THE GENERAL AGREEMENT ON TARIFFS AND TRADE (GATT)

GATT is a regular meeting of countries intent on promoting more free trade and reducing protectionist measures. There have been successive 'rounds' of agreements to reduce protectionist measures like tariffs and quotas. GATT also seeks to gain preferential treatment for less developed countries. GATT has had problems in reducing non-tariff barriers (like governments giving preference to domestic suppliers) and with some countries (Japan) which have complicated internal laws (e.g. anti-pollution requirements) which may reduce imports from other countries. GATT is committed to encouraging free trade and reducing the protectionist measures described on pp.240–1.

EXTENDED WRITING QUESTIONS

1 (*a*) How is the balance of payments on current account calculated?

(*b*) Give three examples of invisible exports by the UK.

(*c*) Why is a current account deficit considered undesirable?

(*d*) What measures can the government adopt to reduce the level of the deficit on current account?

2   (*a*)   What economic benefits can a country derive from international trade?

(*b*)   Describe the main components of balance of payments.

(*c*)   State the arguments for and against restricting imports.

(*d*)   Explain the role of GATT in the international economy.

3   (*a*)   Distinguish between tariffs and quotas as methods of restricting imports.

(*b*)   Describe two other methods (not tariffs or quotas) which may be employed to restrict imports.

(*c*)   (i) Why do some countries attempt to reduce the size of the surplus on their balance of payments?

(ii) What measures can such countries adopt to reduce the size of their balance of payments surplus?

4   (*a*)   Distinguish between

(i) fixed exchange rates

(ii) floating exchange rates.

(*b*)   How may a balance of payments deficit be corrected when a country is operating

(i) fixed exchange rates?

(ii) floating exchange rates?

(*c*)   Give two advantages and two disadvantages of a high sterling exchange rate.

5   (*a*)   Distinguish between

(i) a customs union

(ii) a free trade area.

Give an example of each.

(*b*)   For what economic reasons was the European Community formed?

(*c*)   What have been the economic effects of the UK belonging to the European Community?

(*d*)   What are the main arguments in favour of UK's continued membership of the European Community?

DATA RESPONSE

UK balance of payments

Year	Visible balance £ billion	Invisible balance £ billion	Current balance £ billion	Balance for official financing £ billion
1980	–	+2,028	+3,206	−1,372
1985	−2,068	+5,020	–	+927

(*a*)   (i) What was the visible balance in 1980?

(ii) What was the current balance in 1985?

(*b*)   To which of the following categories, given in the table, would following transactions belong?

(i) A British tourist in Spain pays his hotel bill.

(ii) The sale of Jaguar cars in the USA.

(iii) The flow of interest, profits and dividends into the UK from UK investments overseas.

(c)   Describe the changes in balance of payments between 1980 and 1985.

(d)   How might the government allocate the £927 billion surplus on the balance for official financing in 1985?

(e)   Assume that an economy makes a large balance of payments deficit.

(i) Give three possible causes of this deficit.

(ii) What measures can the government of that country take to reduce the size of the deficit?

Answer

(a)   (i) The visible balance in 1980 was £1,178 billion. This can be calculated from knowing that visible balance + invisible balance = current account balance: 1,178 + 2,028 = 3,206.

(ii) −2,068 + 5,020 = 2,952. The answer is £2,952 billion.

(b)   (i) Invisible import.

(ii) Visible export.

(iii) Invisible export.

(c)   1980 . . . a visible surplus of £1,178 billion plus an invisible surplus of £2,028 billion resulted in a current account surplus of £3,206 billion. However, the balance for official financing was a deficit of £1,372 billion. This implies a large outflow of investment funds on investment and other capital flows.

1985 . . . a visible deficit of £2,068 billion plus an invisible surplus of £5,020 billion resulted in a current account surplus of £2,952. However, the balance for official financing was a surplus of £927 billion, which again implies a significant outflow of funds on investment and other capital flows.

(d)   The surplus can be allocated in three ways:

– add to reserves of gold and foreign currency reserves.

– repay loans made from the IMF and other monetary authorities in previous years.

(e)   (i) Three possible causes of a balance of payments deficit:

– High prices of domestically produced goods (inflation).

– The exchange rate may be too high, meaning that exports are expensive and imports are cheap.

– Low quality of domestically produced goods.

(ii) – Higher interest rates to attract investment to the company.

– Deflationary policies to reduce inflation.

– Lower exchange rate to increase exports and reduce imports.

– Protectionist measures, e.g. tariffs and quotas.

Answers to multiple-choice questions:

MC1	(*a*)	**MC7**	(*a*)
MC2	(*d*)	**MC8**	(*d*)
MC3	(*b*)	**MC9**	(*d*)
MC4	(*c*)	**MC10**	(*b*)
MC5	(*b*)	**MC11**	(*c*)
MC6	(*e*)	**MC12**	(*c*)

EXAMINATION TECHNIQUE

REVISION

Good revision ensures a good examination result – make sure that your revision covers the whole syllabus. This is necessary because the multiple-choice questions may be set on all aspects of the syllabus and essays will cover a wide variety of topics.

You should, if possible, make a thorough study of previous examination papers to make sure that you can answer past questions. In your revision work, practise answering questions and noting down important points, setting yourself a target in a given number of minutes.

SHORT-ANSWER QUESTIONS

These may be the multiple-choice type of question or the open-response short-answer question, perhaps requiring one or two sentences (or even words) in response to the question. Examples of the open-response short-answer question:

1   Name two internal economies of scale.
2   Define opportunity cost.
3   (*a*)   Define a public corporation.
    (*b*)   Give two examples of public corporations.
4   Why is the balancing item included in the balance of payments accounts?

Examiners should have indicated the number of marks being allocated to each question. You will normally be required to answer *all* questions, so do not miss any out. These questions test your recall and knowledge. Read the question carefully and give a relevant and clear answer in response.

MULTIPLE-CHOICE QUESTIONS

1   **Read the instructions closely** If you are required to answer all the questions, then it is important to do this. Make sure that you fill in details of your name, candidate number and centre number correctly.

You will not usually lose marks if you get the answer wrong, but you must ensure that you answer in the correct way. For instance, you may be required to draw a pencil mark vertically or horizontally through the correct alternative letter. Make sure you know what is required.

2 **Read the question thoroughly and closely** There is normally quite a lot of information to consider in any one question, and mistakes can easily be made. For instance, the word *not* in any question can dramatically change your response.

3 **When approaching an individual question** and after reading the information thoroughly, it is normally best to identify the responses it *could not* possibly be. This will leave you with the possible correct answers and you obviously have to make a choice of what you consider to be correct.

4 **If you have no real idea** of what the correct answer is, it is advisable at least to make an attempt.

5 **Be careful not to spend too much time** on certain questions. If you are having problems with a question, leave it and return to it later. Bear in mind that you have a definite time limit which is strictly adhered to by the invigilator.

6 **It is important** to check over your answers, making sure you have answered every question.

Above all, *read* the questions properly and follow the answering instructions.

ESSAY QUESTIONS OR EXTENDED WRITING QUESTIONS

1 **Read the question paper** thoroughly (including the rubric) and decide what questions, and in which order, you are going to answer.

2 **Follow the instructions carefully** Make sure you answer the correct number of questions. On no account should you answer more or less than the required number of questions. Examiners will ignore any questions above the required number. If you do not answer enough questions, you will obviously limit the marks it is possible for you to obtain. Make sure you know which questions are compulsory and which questions involve an element of choice between questions.

3 **You must be careful** not to spend too much time on any particular questions, even if you feel that you could spend more. If you do, it means you have less time to spend on the others and you are likely to lose marks by not explaining the details adequately.

4 **Always plan your response briefly** for a minute or so before answering. This will give your answers an organization and structure and will ensure you do not forget to include some points.

5 **Attempt those questions** you know best at the outset, whilst you are fresh. Again, remember not to spend too much time on the questions you know best.

6 **Make sure you answer** the question set. The information in the essay must be relevant to the particular question. You will not get any marks for information which is not relevant, no matter how correct or well-written the information is. Avoid all irrelevant detail. It is sometimes a good idea to include a sketch or drawing within the framework of your answer to emphasize a particular point.

7 **Where you have to make calculations,** always show the working and detail. In this way you will receive some marks, even if you get the final answer wrong.

8 **Always read over** what you have written. Make any necessary corrections and omit anything which does not make sense.

9 **Pay attention to details** of style of English. It is important that your essay is well organized, with paragraphs. Spelling and punctuation should be of a good standard. Above all, make sure that you answer the correct number of questions and answer the question which is set.

10 **Extended writing questions** will be structured, and some are data-based. 'Structured' means that there are many parts to the questions (a, b, c, d), possibly increasing in level of difficulty. Each part should have allocated to it a number of marks. You must take these marks into account when answering the question – you will need to write in more detail for a part which gives more marks. For instance if part (*a*) gives 2 marks and part (*d*) 10 marks, you will need to include more detail in response to part (*d*).

Data-based means that the extended writing question is based perhaps on statistics or a prose passage. These are very similar to data-response questions.

11 **Once you have decided** what information is relevant to the question, you need to decide how the examiner wishes you to deal with it (i.e. in great detail or perhaps just one or two lines of definition). Here are some words often used in questions by examiners, with a brief indication on how you should approach such questions:

Outline – this implies brevity, and you should give only the important details.

Describe – just a straightforward account or description is needed.

Define – state exactly the meaning of a word, phrase or concept.

Explain or account for – detailed and coherent coverage, giving reasons to explain your response.

Analyse – again implies a detailed response and explanation of relationships between variables.

Assess – you need to evaluate the value of a statement or other variable. This may involve arguments for and against.

Discuss or examine – detailed investigation needed, with arguments for or against.

Illustrate – here you need to explain something with the use of examples.

Compare or distinguish – an instruction to show the similarities and differences between variables.

State or list – a command to do something which will be self-explanatory from the question.

12   **Within the structured extended writing questions** there will be a relationship between those structured parts of the question giving more marks with possibly words such as 'explain', 'account for', 'analyse', 'assess', 'discuss' or 'examine', somewhere in the question.

   Also, those structured parts of the questions giving relatively few marks will possibly have words such as 'define', 'outline' somewhere in the question.

DATA-RESPONSE QUESTIONS

1   In this type of question you will be presented with economic data in some form and you will be asked to interpret it and use it as a basis for economic analysis.

2   The aim of data-response questions is to test your understanding of economic principles and theory and your ability to apply this to specific questions. The objective is to make relevant your study of Economics to real world and relevant questions.

3   A data-response question may be presented in one of five main forms:
   (a)   statistical tables
   (b)   graphs
   (c)   pie charts
   (d)   photographs
   (e)   prose passage – from a book or newspaper.

4   Read the data carefully several times. Make a list of relevant points. When presented with a statistical table or graph, always look for patterns in the data.

5   As far as possible, use economic concepts in your analysis. Do not describe when you should analyse the data (refer back to the meanings of these terms).

6   Much of the advice on how to answer extended writing questions applies here. I would like to repeat the advice to be relevant at all times and not to include detail which is not required. Also allocate your time sensibly, not only between questions (i.e. do not spend too much time on one question) but also within questions. By this is meant that many of the data-response questions are structured and the techniques discussed in point **10** on extended writing questions need to be reread.

PREPARING FOR THE EXAMINATION

It has already been mentioned that revision is vital to ensure a good examination result. Some weeks before the examination you should plan a revision timetable to make sure that you have enough time to revise all the required topics. Your notes should be of good quality, which will be of great help when revising. Read through these slowly and thoroughly and understand the important ideas. You should have copies of past papers to help you in your revision. Practise doing the different types of question.

Remember that a good result does not depend on luck, it depends on hard work and good planning.

INDEX